100 THINGS TO DO IN EUGENE BEFORE YOU DIE

100 THINGS TO DO IN EUGENE BEFORE YOU DIE

JULIE FURST HENNING

Reedy Press
PO Box 5131
St. Louis, MO 63139, USA
www.reedypress.com

Library of Congress Control Number: 2017957320

ISBN: 9781681061269

Design by Jill Halpin

Photo Credits: All images provided by author unless otherwise indicated.

Printed in the United States of America
18 19 20 21 22   5 4 3 2 1

Please note that websites, phone numbers, addresses, and company names are subject to change or cancellation. We did our best to relay the most accurate information available, but due to circumstances beyond our control, please do not hold us liable for misinformation. When exploring new destinations, please do your homework before you go.

DEDICATION

To my parents for taking slow and immersive vacations. To my three children for being excellent travel companions. To my sister for always having my back. To my Aunt Ginny for unconditional love. And to all my weird friends (you know who you are) for many crazy and awesome memories.

CONTENTS

Music and Entertainment

Sports and Recreation

Culture and History

Shopping and Fashion

PREFACE

When I tell people why I love living in Eugene, Oregon, I point and say, "Mountains that way. Ocean the other way." Nestled in the heart of the Southern Willamette Valley, Eugene is perhaps best known for craft beer, pinot noir, the University of Oregon, and track and field. But it's really a high quality of life and a temperate climate that draw and keep people here. Whether you love to run, mountain bike, hike, sail, surf, or ski, year-round outdoor recreation will keep you healthy and happy as much as your heart desires. Then mix in a thriving technology scene, a vibrant art community, and close proximity to sustainable and local agriculture, and you have a recipe for a happy life.

Because of the all-around general awesomeness of this corner of the Earth, I had a difficult time narrowing down the list of recommendations for this book. I found myself constantly adding, modifying, and updating the table of contents based on suggestions and ideas from small business owners, authorities in local tourism, and many people who were born and raised here in Eugene and Springfield. In the end, I came to the conclusion that one hundred ideas gives readers a great jumping-off point for their own deep exploration of the Emerald Valley.

Happy trails!

PRE
5-30-75
R.I.P.
"PRE"
For your dedication and loyalty
To your principles and beliefs...
For your love, warmth, and friendship
For your family and friends...
You are missed by so many,
And you will never be forgotten...
FOR A GREAT GUY
follow your heart
E3599

ACKNOWLEDGMENTS

A nod to Stephen Hoshaw, PR and social media manager at Travel Lane County, for assisting me with this entire project, including answering my many emails. And a "high five" to everyone else who provided me with input, ideas, and support as I plugged along on this project.

FOOD AND DRINK

1

GRAZE YOUR WAY THROUGH "THE WHIT"

Named in honor of John Whiteaker, Oregon's first governor, Eugene's Whiteaker neighborhood is a mix of single-family homes, restaurants, and businesses. Running west of the Washington-Jefferson Street Bridge, east of Chambers Street, north of West Sixth Avenue, and south of the Willamette River, "the Whit" was once primarily thought of as a blue-collar working-class neighborhood. Today, the area is a destination for craft beer, slow food, and all-around eccentricity. Blair Boulevard cuts diagonally through the heart of the dining and entertainment scene, with popular stops ranging from Tacovore to Papa's Soul Food Kitchen and BBQ, Blairally Arcade, Sam Bond's Garage, Board, and Grit Kitchen and Wine. Food trucks typically occupy the corner of West Third Avenue and Van Buren Street, within earshot of live entertainment on the outdoor patio at the Ninkasi Brewing tasting room. Within easy walking distance are Hop Valley Brewing, Beergarden, and the Oakshire Public House—all stops on the Eugene Ale Trail.

TIP

Parking in the Whit can be tricky on a Friday or Saturday night; walk, bike, or carpool and anticipate long lines at nearly all the restaurants.

2

FILL YOUR CELLAR
WHILE PLAYING PINOT BINGO

Climate, rainfall, soil, terrain, and tradition affect the taste of a glass of wine. In the Southern Willamette Valley, these factors play in favor of pinot noir, and wine enthusiasts from near and far come to test their own palates. With more than twenty vineyards within a twenty-mile drive of the Eugene-Springfield area, friends tend to congregate on south-facing slopes with picnic baskets, blankets, and uncorked bottles of estate wine. A passport-style game in the theme of the Eugene Ale Trail, Pinot Bingo encourages visitors to experience regional diversity in wines and in tasting rooms. Blank game cards are available at participating wineries; the Eugene, Cascades, and Coast Visitor Center in Springfield; or the Visitor Information Center in Eugene. The more stamps you earn, the more prizes you win. Complete a row in any direction (a flight) and earn a signed art print from local artist Robert Canaga. Fill the three center columns (a bottle) for a souvenir Riedel Oregon pinot noir glass. Or fill the entire card (full cellar) to be entered in a grand prize drawing. Designated restaurants, bakeries, wine bars, and public houses help to fill in the blanks with "pairing" stamps. Prizes may be redeemed at the Eugene, Cascades, and Coast Visitor Center in Springfield.

eugenecascadescoast.org/wine-country/pinot-bingo

3

FIND THE PERFECT PINT
ON THE EUGENE ALE TRAIL

The Willamette Valley may be known for its vineyards, but the same rich soil, mild climate, and abundant rainfall result in favorable growing conditions for the hop vine. Provide award-winning brewers with excellent base ingredients and access to ultra-pure water from the McKenzie River, and the outcome is great regional diversity in breweries and beer. Following the Eugene Ale Trail, guests pick up a passport booklet at any of eighteen participating breweries; the Eugene, Cascades, and Coast Visitor Center in Springfield; or the Visitor Information Center in Eugene. The trail passes through breweries and tasting rooms in downtown Eugene and Springfield and out to Agrarian Ales in Coburg and the Brewers Union Local 180 in Oakridge. Each location has something different on tap, with several venues offering appetizers or a full menu (some destinations allow pets and children, but confirm this in advance before setting out on a family adventure). Passports with eight (or more) stamps may be redeemed for an official sixty-four-ounce Eugene Ale Trail growler, with an additional stainless-steel cup for guests who frequent the Brewers Union in Oakridge.

eugenecascadescoast.org/eugene-ale-trail

4

DELIGHT IN A GREEN EUGENE AT THE SATURDAY MARKET

A weekly event running rain or shine every Saturday between early April and mid-November, the Lane County Farmers Market/Saturday Market typically draws a crowd to the intersection of Eighth Avenue and Oak Street in downtown Eugene. It is technically two separate events, with farmers on one side and artisans and makers on the other. Plan to spend several hours walking among the endless rows of booths of locally made, handcrafted wares and stalls of the freshest "farm to table" produce. On the far end, the International Food Court houses fifteen outdoor restaurants. Located near the Market Stage is a showcase for local talent, with six different acts performing every Saturday. Running along the perimeter are face painters, balloon artists, and spontaneous singers with ribbons on their tambourines. Check out this quintessential "Green Eugene" market experience if you are downtown on a Saturday between 9 a.m. and 3 p.m.

Intersection of Eighth Ave. and Oak St.
lanecountyfarmersmarket.org

5

HOOK THE CATCH OF THE DAY

AT FISHERMAN'S MARKET

Owned and operated by Ryan and Debbie Rogers, a commercial fishing family with roots in Alaska, Fisherman's Market specializes in the "boat to table" dining experience. Capitalizing on its close proximity to the Pacific Ocean and the Columbia River Gorge, customers enjoy a wide variety of fresh-caught, wild seafood that varies by the weather and the season. It was featured on the popular television show *Diners, Drive-Ins, and Dives*, and host Guy Fieri enjoyed Dungeness crab transferred from the live tank and steamed to perfection in the crab pot running just outside the front door. Fisherman's Market boasts the best fish and chips in Eugene, and any type of seafood may be paired with fries and coleslaw, not just cod. Indoor and covered outdoor seating is available; the kitchen uses a "take a number" ordering system to keep the line moving (orders are broadcast over a speaker system and picked up at the front counter).

830 W Seventh Ave.
541-484-2722
eugenefishmarket.com

6

DRINK A BEER AFTER SHOPPING FOR HOPS
AT BEERGARDEN

A one-of-a-kind business model that unites green thumbs with heads of foam, Eugene's Beergarden is located at the intersection of hops and horticulture—quite literally next to Gray's Garden Center. With forty-two types of beer on tap and hundreds of bottles of craft beer, wine, cider, and kombucha, beergarden has one of the largest selections of adult beverages in town. Patrons have two options for dining: (1) a collection of tabletops and standalone tables in the ornate and more intimate indoor dining room or (2) long rows of family-style picnic tables on the covered back patio. Running the perimeter of the back lot are local food trucks serving a variety of affordable food. Beergarden hosts several forms of entertainment throughout the week, from trivia night to live music ranging from honkey-tonk to classic old-time rock and roll.

777 W Sixth Ave.
541-505-9432
beergardenme.com

7

ORDER A BAG O' BURGERS

AT BOB'S BURGER EXPRESS

Founded in 1955 and known for its nineteen cent burgers, Bob's Burgers was once a hyper-regional chain across Salem, Eugene, Springfield, Corvallis, Junction City, Bend, and Redmond. Re-opened at 2766 West Eleventh Avenue in 2016, the new Bob's Burger Express seeks to re-create the 1950s experience by using the original yellow and red circular logo and featuring many of the most popular classic menu items on the express menu. Inside the dining room, a "remember when . . ." wall and framed photographs showcase the restaurant's history, from the original marquee to old menus; past promotions; and photos of employees, customers, and even company mascots from across the decades. Highlights of a trip to Bob's range from a root-beer milkshake to a Bag O' Burgers: six classic burgers bundled together for $9.99. But don't forget to add a cup of secret sauce for an additional eighty cents; it's made from the original top-secret recipe.

2766 W Eleventh Ave.
541-505-9815

8

EMBARK ON A PEDAL-POWERED PUB CRAWL

AT PACIFIC PUB CYCLE

While Eugene does not yet have fleets of Lyft or Uber drivers waiting to carry residents around town, Pacific Pub Cycle presents a unique way to travel between downtown breweries and tap houses. Departing from and returning to the Fifth Street Public Market, up to fourteen people board the "pub cycle," a community-pedaled bicycle steered by a licensed driver. Typically following a pre-determined route, groups make about five stops over a period of two hours for beer, wine, cider, or craft cocktails. Tours run rain or shine, and a minimum of eight people is required on a single reservation. Note: beverages are consumed at the stops and not served or consumed along the way.

541-632-4343
pacificpubcycle.com

9

FIND MAGIC IN THE HOLE
AT VOODOO DOUGHNUT

Channeling the general "weirdness" of Portland, Voodoo Doughnut's third location in Oregon is well suited to Eugene. Breaking the stereotypical doughnut mold, Voodoo Doughnut features such creations as the Pot Hole, Dirty Snowball, Mango Tango, Memphis Mafia, and triple-cream filled Cock-N-Balls. Not to be missed is the trademark voodoo doll doughnut filled with raspberry jelly and pierced by a pretzel stake. With more than fifty choices on the menu, doughnuts come in three general categories: raised yeast, cake, and vegan. Known for its famous pink packaging, the Voodoo credo is "good things come in pink boxes." Voodoo patrons may also purchase calorie-free merchandise, including bumper stickers, underpants, coffee mugs, and a variety of old and new music recorded and produced under the Voodoo Doughnut Recordings label (and coincidentally the world's leading doughnut-based recording company).

20 E Broadway
541-868-8666
voodoodoughnut.com

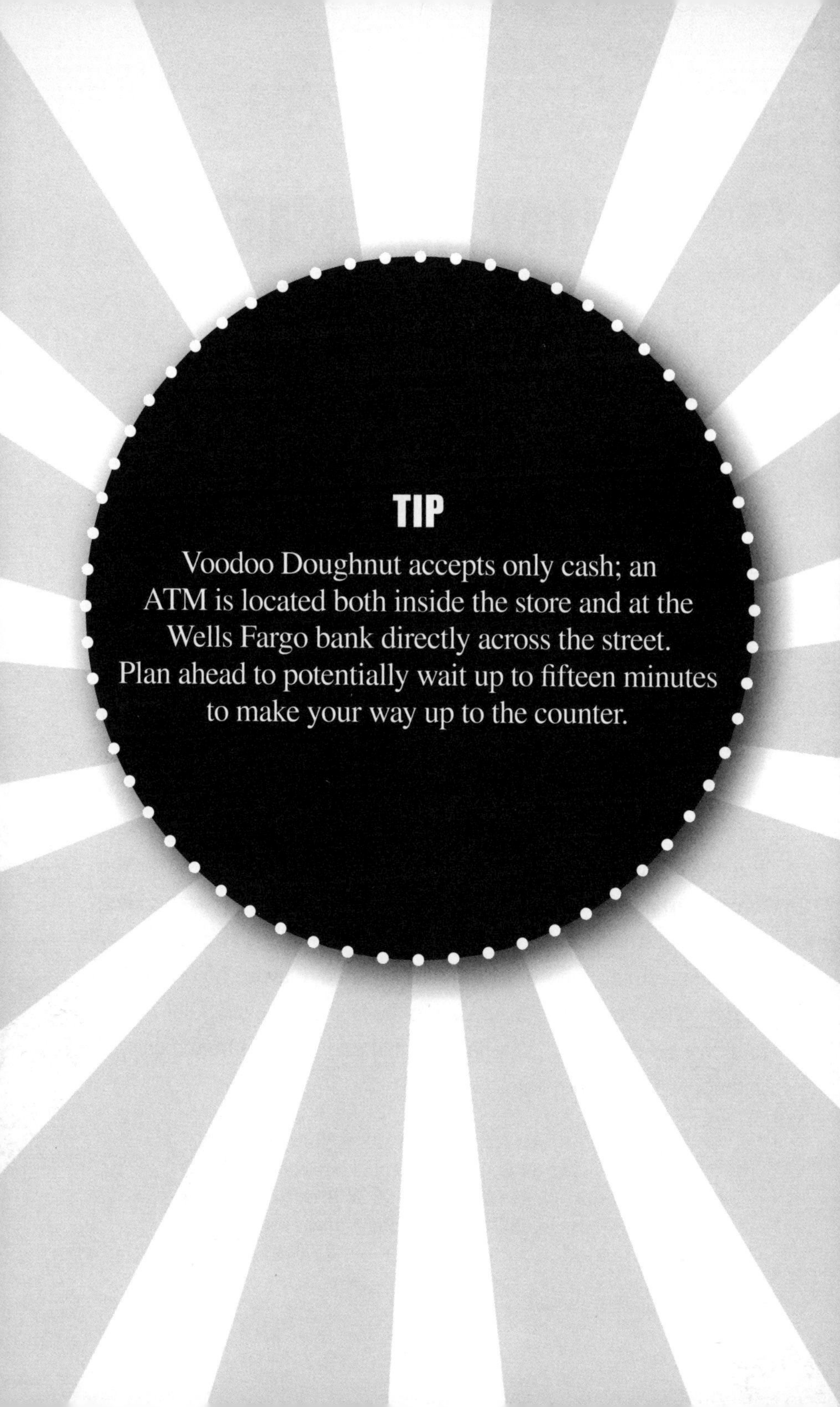

TIP

Voodoo Doughnut accepts only cash; an ATM is located both inside the store and at the Wells Fargo bank directly across the street. Plan ahead to potentially wait up to fifteen minutes to make your way up to the counter.

10

ENJOY GOURMET ICE CREAM

AT PRINCE PUCKLER'S AND RED WAGON CREAMERY

A local favorite for more than forty years, Prince Puckler's gourmet ice cream has been welcoming families to the corner of Nineteenth and Agate since 1975. It was visited by President Barack Obama and First Lady Michelle Obama in 2008, and now mint chip may also be ordered simply as Obama's Favorite. Available in cups, cones, milkshakes, or sundaes, handmade ice cream flavors range from Pistachio Almond to Tiger Stripes and Red Raspberry Cheesecake, along with the traditional favorites. A few blocks south of the University of Oregon campus, Prince Puckler's is known to lure in the college crowd. An equally delicious counterpart, Red Wagon Creamery has made its mark on Eugene's sweet tooth. What started in a child's little red wagon grew to a food cart and is now Oregon's smallest dairy plant—a two-hundred-square-foot small-batch ice creamery in the heart of the West Broadway shopping, dining, and entertainment district. Flavor choices at Red Wagon Creamery range from Hail to the Bee to Smoked Salt Caramel and Not-So-Plain-Jane Vanilla; seasonal and regional ingredients are sourced whenever possible.

Prince Puckler's Ice Cream, 1605 E Nineteenth Ave.
541-344-4418, princepucklers.com
Red Wagon Creamery, 55 W Broadway
541-345-8008, redwagoncreamery.com

FINE DINE ON A DIME
AT LCC'S RENAISSANCE ROOM RESTAURANT

A fine-dining opportunity at a fraction of the cost, the Renaissance Room restaurant at the Lane Community College (LCC) main campus is one of the best-kept secrets of Eugene's restaurant scene. It is staffed by second-year culinary arts and hospitality management students, who receive real-world experience while working under the close supervision of their course instructors and program advisors. Patrons can expect dining menus that change regularly based on the students' current focus of study; whenever possible ingredients are sourced locally and sustainably, with an emphasis on the growing season and availability. And the best part? Lunch is only twelve dollars and includes a choice of soup or salad, entree, and a dessert sampler (beverages are an additional two dollars).

4000 E Thirtieth Ave.
541-463-3503
lanecc.edu/culinary/renaissance-room

TIP

The Renaissance Room is only open for lunch and only open during the fall, winter, and spring terms. Advance reservations are required and must be made via email: renroom@lanecc.edu.

12

GO ON A HUNT
FOR THE HIDEAWAY BAKERY

Tucked behind Mazzi's Italian restaurant in South Eugene, Hideaway Bakery is a "hidden" gem serving up Old World-style artisan bread, homemade pastries, wood-fired pizza, and handcrafted pastas. A large masonry hearth occupies the center of the bakery and is fueled with recycled wood from a local mill. While indoor seating is available in a large, comfortable space, the covered patio is a popular choice in warmer weather. Families with toddlers tend to congregate at the tables closer to the sandbox play area. A community hub as much as a dining spot, Hideaway Bakery is also popular for its year-round farmers market running Saturdays from 9 a.m. to 2 p.m. You may also see long lines at the Hideaway Bakery booth at the Downtown Farmers Market between May and October. Thursdays are wood-oven pizza nights all summer long; local musicians are likely to be in attendance. After the calorie consumption has concluded, cross Amazon Drive and walk the Rexius Trail loop all the way to Frank Kinney Park.

3377 E Amazon Dr.
541-868-1982
hideawaybakery.com

AFTER YOU FIND HIDEAWAY, FIND THESE OTHER DESTINATIONS:

Barry's Bakery and Deli
Southtowne Shoppes
2805 Oak St.
541-343-6444
barrysbakery.blogspot.com

Metropol Bakery
2538 Willamette St.
541-465-4730
metropolbakery.com

Noisette Pastry Kitchen
200 W Broadway
541-654-5257
noisettepk.com

Sweet Life Patisserie
755 Monroe St.
541-683-5676
sweetlifedesserts.com

13

DINE IN AN ELECTRIC RAIL CAR

AT THE OREGON ELECTRIC STATION

Before Amtrak built a train station in Eugene's Market District, the Oregon Electric Railway carried passengers between Eugene and Portland on an electric railway. Refurbished and restored to its original 1914 splendor, the building is registered and protected as a National Historic Landmark. While passenger service on the railway was discontinued in May 1933 and the building had many tenants throughout the years, it is currently home to the Oregon Electric Station restaurant, a venue known for its upscale dining and romantically classical ambiance. Dining options range from a seasonal outdoor patio and an elegant bar and lounge to sit-down service in one of two original, retrofitted electric rail cars.

27 E Fifth Ave.
541-485-4444
oesrestaurant.com

TIP

This spot is popular for holiday parties and corporate events, so dining reservations are recommended for large groups and anyone celebrating a special event.

AMP UP YOUR DAY
AT PUTTERS PIZZA AND FAMILY ENTERTAINMENT CENTER

Because Eugene gets an average of forty-six inches of annual rainfall, Putters Pizza and Family Entertainment Center is a popular spot for indoor recreation. Housed in a fifty-thousand-square-foot facility, Putters features an eighteen-hole miniature golf course, a multi-level laser tag arena, an arcade, a billiards room, playground structures, and enough seating for groups of up to five hundred people. Worth noting is discounted mini golf on Tuesdays and a price drop in laser tag each Thursday (from $11 to $6 per game). Pizza, salad, and appetizers are offered to dining patrons, with a large selection of local craft beer and cider on tap. Strike City Lanes, one of a handful of local bowling alleys, is located in the same complex. Discounts for Putters Pizza and Family Entertainment Center and Strike City Lanes are typically printed on the same page in the monthly coupon circular sent out to residents in the US mail.

1156 State Highway 99 N
541-688-8901

RIDE THE CAROUSEL
AT ROARING RAPIDS PIZZA COMPANY

Roaring Rapids Pizza Company has provided families with great pizza and fond memories for decades. Built along the southern bank of the Willamette River in the patch of land where Eugene blends into Springfield, Roaring Rapids is particularly popular with the birthday party crowd. Surrounded by arcade games and candy machines, the central attraction in the pavilion room is a free ride on the authentic 1931 C. W. Parker musical carousel. Eat in one of two indoor dining areas, or venture out to the back patio for views of the river's roaring rapids. The weekday Rapid Pizza Lunch Buffet presents patrons with the opportunity to sample a variety of award-winning pizzas for less than ten dollars. While the restaurant's mascot, Brownie the Bear, usually sits at a piano near the main entrance, he occasionally comes to life for parties and special events.

4006 Franklin Blvd.
541-988-9819
roaringrapidspizza.com

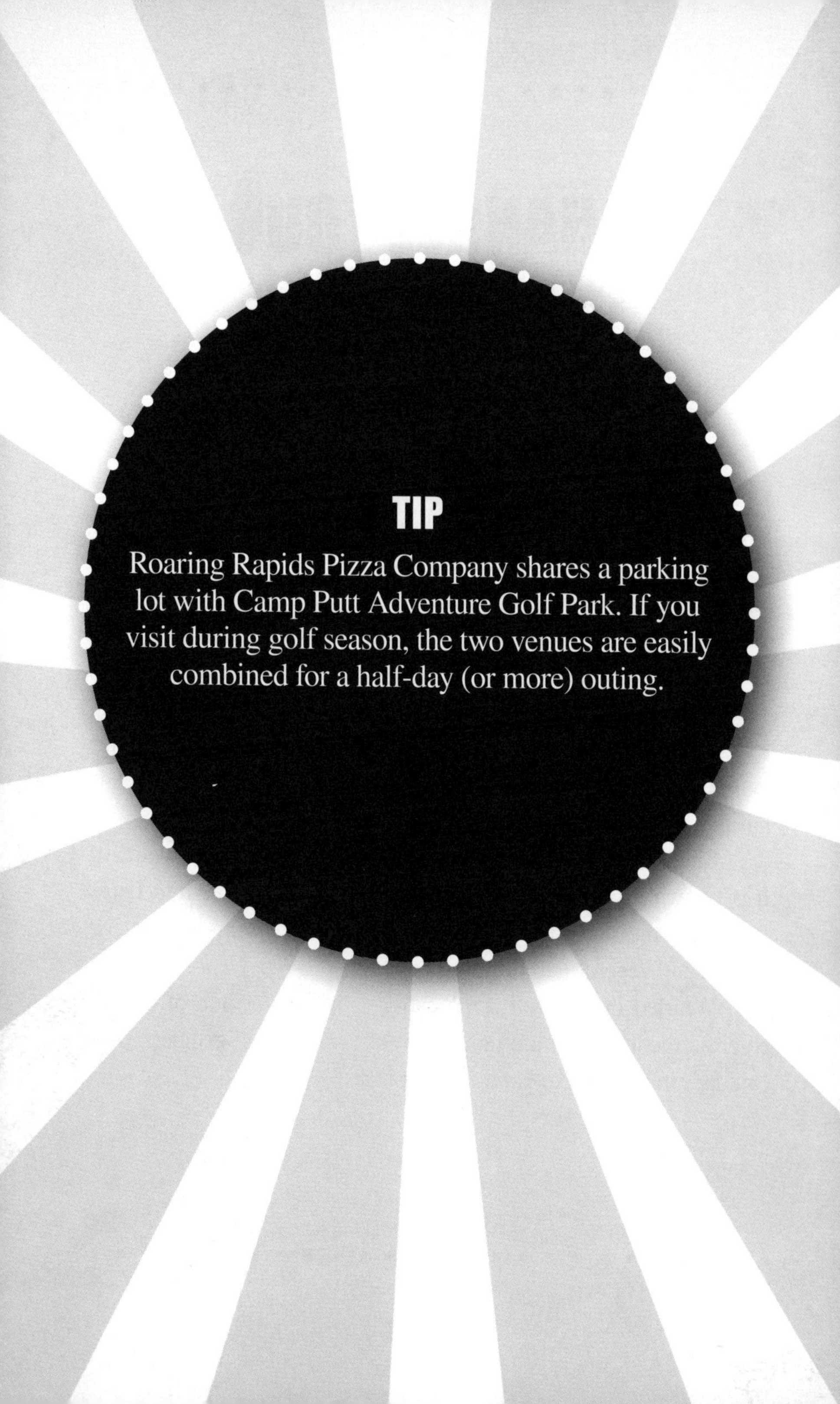

TIP

Roaring Rapids Pizza Company shares a parking lot with Camp Putt Adventure Golf Park. If you visit during golf season, the two venues are easily combined for a half-day (or more) outing.

16

CHANNEL YOUR INNER ITALIAN
AT A LOCAL PIZZERIA

Like any reputable college town, Eugene has a variety of places to order and enjoy pizza, from chains to holes in the wall. Channel your inner Italian and work your way through this list of independently owned local establishments.

Track Town, close to campus, is an old-school pizzeria established in 1977. Pizzas are named after athletic events and range from the Decathalon to the 100 Yard Dash.

Mezza Luna specializes in by-the-slice pizza served all day long, with a wide variety of meat and vegetarian pizzas on the menu. Winner of multiple "readers' choice" and best of Eugene awards, it has two locations in Eugene and one in Springfield.

Sizzle Pie is a primetime pizzeria in the heart of downtown. It is known for its trendy ambiance and its slogan: Death to False Pizza. By-the-slice and full pies are available, with options for vegans and vegetarians.

Whirled Pies downtown location is a popular hub of music, entertainment, and community events. It serves grinders and calzones in addition to hand-tossed pizzas.

Expanding from the original 1989 campus location, Pegasus Pizza has grown to three locations in Eugene. It specializes in hand-tossed, brick-oven pies, with an extensive list of meats, cheeses, and vegetables on the "build your own" menu.

Pizza Research Institute specializes in vegan pizzas at a quaint indoor/outdoor space in the heart of the Whiteaker neighborhood. It is only open for dinner.

Track Town
1809 Franklin Blvd.
541-284-8484
tracktownoncampus.com

Mezza Luna
Downtown Eugene
933 Pearl St.
541-684-8900

Mezza Luna
Crescent Village
2776 Shadow View Dr.
541-743-2999

Mezza Luna
Downtown Springfield
115 S Fifth St.
541-653-8661
mezzalunapizzeria.com

Sizzle Pie
910 Willamette St.
541-683-7437
sizzlepie.com

Whirled Pies
199 W Eighth Ave.
541-338-9333
whirledpies.com

Pegasus Pizza
Campus
790 E Fourteenth Ave.
541-344-4471

Pegasus Pizza
Oakway
4 Oakway Center
541-344-0844

Pegasus Pizza
South Eugene
2864 Willamette St. #300
541-344-9931
pegasuspizza.net

Pizza Research Institute
325 Blair Blvd.
541-343-1307
pripizza.com

17

SURROUND YOURSELF WITH MEMORABILIA

FROM 1950S ADDI'S DINER

The decor at Addi's Diner in Springfield is a step back in time to the heyday of the 1950s, from gingham tablecloths to a jukebox and floor-to-celling memorabilia ranging from Betty Boop to old license plates. The nostalgic and eclectic corner diner has developed a reputation for massive portions of comfort food. From the Big Plate Pancake (a pancake the size of a pizza) to the Frenchy (cinnamon-roll French toast), portion sizes are plentiful enough to split an order between two or more people. Addi's is open for lunch and dinner and is located at the corner of South Second Street and South A Street, dining space is intimate, and the parking lot is small. Look for a red and white building with a matching convertible on the exterior wall.

207 S A St., Springfield
541-747-9482

18

TRY TOFU OR TEMPEH
AT SURATA SOYFOODS

Celebrating forty years serving the Eugene community, Surata Soyfoods specializes in organic tofu and tempeh. With distribution across Oregon and Washington and into Idaho and Montana, Surata's "bean meat" helps support the palate of the vegetarian and vegan communities. For retail purchases, Surata Soyfoods is open to the general public only on Tuesday and Thursday between 11 a.m. and 5:15 p.m. During this time, fresh tofu and frozen tempeh sold from the small front-office retail space are discount-priced overruns and odd cuts, which are less than perfect but still perfectly healthy.

325 W Third Ave.
541-485-6990
suratasoy.com

TIP

Bring your own cooler and ice packs for transporting frozen goods.

19

EAT EVERYTHING ON A WAFFLE

AT OFF THE WAFFLE

Sweeter than a traditional Belgian waffle, Liège Belgian waffles are perfect for breakfast or dessert. Crunchy on the outside, with a mouthwatering, fluffy middle, Liège waffles melt during the rising process to form a crispy, caramelized crust. As the name implies, waffles are the signature menu item at Off the Waffle, a family-owned café with two Eugene locations. Ranging from savory to sweet, everything on the Off the Waffle menu is served atop a freshly baked waffle, with emphasis on locally sourced ingredients and 100 percent organic produce.

840 Willamette St.
541-632-4225

2540 Willamette St.
541-632-4316
offthewaffle.com

TIP

Off the Waffle is open seven days per week, but weekends are particularly great for business. Expect to wait for a table if you arrive during prime brunch hours.

20

BULK UP ON ORGANIC FOOD

AT HUMMINGBIRD WHOLESALE

Eugene's family-owned organic food distributor, Hummingbird Wholesale specializes in seeds, pasta, beans, legumes, oils, spices, dried fruits, nut butter, chocolate, granola, honey, and even animal feed. Tapping into a network of local and regional agriculture, Hummingbird's focus is on sustainability, quality, and ethical and long-term working relationships. It offers membership-based discount pricing to restaurants and grocery stores, but the general public is welcome (and encouraged) to "bulk up" in the retail storefront between 8 a.m. and 4 p.m., Monday through Friday. Arrive hungry, as many items have free samples!

150 Shelton-McMurphey Blvd.
541-686-0921
hummingbirdwholesale.com

TIP
For more local bulk food options, consider shopping at any of these local, independent grocery stores: the Kiva Grocery, Sundance Natural Foods, Red Barn Natural Grocery, Capella Market, Friendly Street Market, and New Frontier Market.

MUSIC AND ENTERTAINMENT

21

BUST A MOVE
AT EUGENE'S LARGEST DANCE PARTY

Eugene's largest annual dance party for the past five years running, the Mega Dance Party was conceived and planned by sixteen friends who simply love to dance without the distraction of speeches and fundraising. Held in March in the upstairs ballroom of the Veterans Memorial Association (Vets Club) building, the event has grown to an average of four hundred to five hundred people over the course of five hours of non-stop music ranging from '70s funk and '80s new wave to current Billboard hits. Highlights of the party include glow-in-the-dark bling, free coat check, and a cash bar—a ten dollar per person cover charge pays for the DJ and snacks, with any extra money split between local charities, including the Relief Nursery, Eugene Education Fund, White Bird Clinic, and Centro Latino Americano. Event dates, details, and photos from previous years are posted on the Mega Dance Party Eugene Facebook page.

1626 Willamette St.

SAY HELLO TO THE HERD
AT ARAGON ALPACAS

Marked by a wooden sign painted to match the barn and outbuildings, Aragon Alpacas is a whimsical midway point of interest between Eugene and Creswell. Happy to graze in the rolling hills of the South Willamette Valley, herds of adorable alpacas are easy to spot in their home just off Dillard Road. Known for fine fleece in dark colors, Aragon alpacas receive the finest of care from owners Ann and Mike Dockendorf. Frequently welcoming visitors, school groups, and alpaca farmers from near and far, the Dockendorfs also schedule Open Farm Days throughout the year (the general public is generally welcome at other times, but it's best to call ahead). When sufficiently satiated with alpaca trivia and possibly an animal encounter or two, guests are welcome to frequent A Spinner's Barn farm store and boutique. The small retail store features hand-spun wool, knit items of clothing, patterns, and handicrafts and paintings made by local artistans.

33005 Dillard Rd.
541-912-0782
aragonalpacas.com

23

FEED THE GOATS
AT LONE PINE FARMS

A family-owned farm stand located just north of Eugene, Lone Pine Farms features seasonal produce; dried goods; baking mixes; and jams, butters, and syrups in its indoor marketplace. Kids love this wholesome, family-friendly destination for its playground, swings, slides, sandbox, and fall-themed activities ranging from a corn maze to a pumpkin patch and hayrides pulled by a team of draft horses. The farm's petting barn is home to sheep, bunnies, and a chicken coop with an observation deck to watch the hens nesting. A highlight of the visit is the large goat pen complete with elevated goat walk, where kids delight in using a pulley-and-lever system to raise cups of food pellets into a metal feeding station.

91909 River Rd., Junction City
541-688-4389
lonepinefarms.com

TAKE IN TWELVE HOURS OF MUSIC

AT THE WILLAMETTE VALLEY MUSIC FESTIVAL

For one day each year, the heart of the University of Oregon is transformed into a festival focused on music and the arts. Coordinated by students for students and the greater community, performances run across three stages from noon to midnight, with workshops running at the Erb Memorial Union throughout the day. Musical genres range from folk to hip-hop, indie pop, rock, and reggae—more than twenty bands made this year's lineup. The Willamette Valley Music Festival is free and open to the general public.

1395 University of Oregon
213 EMU
541-346-4373
wvmf.uoregon.edu

25

EXPERIENCE LIVE MUSIC
THROUGHOUT DOWNTOWN

If a vibrant, independent music scene is your thing, downtown Eugene won't let you down. Start with these four key venues, all within an easy walk of the downtown business district, and branch out depending on your budget and your mood.

Woodmen of the World (WOW) Hall, formerly the Woodmen of the World lodge, added the WOW Hall building to the National Register of Historic Places in 1996. Beyond live music, WOW Hall is used for community classes, workshops, lectures, meetings, rehearsals, and recording sessions.

Opened in 1925 as a community theater and later converted to a music house, McDonald Theatre has since been converted to a theater for the performing arts. Regularly on the calendar of events are concerts, lectures, movies, and community gatherings.

Hi-Fi Music Hall is an indoor-outdoor venue for live music and social gatherings. Hi-Fi offers a range of food and alcohol. Shows run six nights a week.

The Jazz Station is an all-ages rehearsal and performance space for musicians and jazz fans The Jazz Station is a membership-based resource for the community. Concerts and performances are open to the general public, with full details on the website.

Woodmen of the World Hall
291 W Eighth Ave.
541-687-2746
wowhall.org

McDonald Theatre
1010 Willamette St.
541-345-4442
mcdonaldtheatre.com

Hi-Fi Music Hall
44 E Seventh Ave.
541-636-3292
hifimusichall.com

The Jazz Station
124 W Broadway
458-205-1030
thejazzstation.org

26

EAT AND BE MERRY
AT KESEY SQUARE

Thought to be the geographic heart of Eugene, Kesey Square has been the site of many culturally significant events throughout the city's history. Named in memory of Ken Kesey, the former area resident and University of Oregon alum best known for authoring *One Flew Over the Cuckoo's Nest*, modern day Kesey Square remains a popular community gathering place. At the center of the red brick lot, a bronze statue of an elderly Kesey reading to his three grandchildren is typically surrounded by an eclectic mix of businesspeople, families with children, musicians, performers, dancers, and artists. In warm weather, a group of food trucks provides a variety of cuisines for the lunch and dinner crowd. As part of with the EUGfun! program, events such as outdoor movie nights, chess matches, and cultural festivals are scheduled at Kesey Square throughout the year.

Intersection of East Broadway and Willamette Street
Downtown Eugene

27

COMBINE OPEN AIR AND MUSIC

AT CUTHBERT AMPHITHEATER'S SYMPHONY IN THE PARK

Summer evenings in Eugene are generally pleasant: warm and free of rain. When presented with the opportunity to enjoy a free symphonic concert in an outdoor setting, residents come out in droves to attend the annual Symphony in the Park. A widely anticipated mid-summer event held at the Cuthbert Amphitheater in the heart of Alton Baker Park, Symphony in the Park encourages blankets and chairs on the lawn. Local food and wine vendors line the perimeter of the grounds, along with activities such as a symphonic "petting zoo" with instruments (not animals) that can be played by curious patrons. Musical performances range from Broadway show tunes to pops and classical favorites. Symphony in the Park to all ages, and admission is free but requires a ticket (a total of four tickets are granted per household, and the event typically sells out quickly). Seating capacity at the Cuthbert Amphitheater is 5,000 and all seats are general admission for this event; a range of outdoor concerts run all summer long at the amphitheater (check the website for a complete musical lineup).

601 Day Island Rd.
541-762-8099
thecuthbert.com

28

WATCH CLASSICAL OR RENEGADE BALLET

AT THE HULT CENTER FOR THE PERFORMING ARTS

Among the most well-traveled ballet ensembles in the United States, the Eugene Ballet Company visits an average of five Western states and performs *The Nutcracker* more than twenty-five times each season. On stage at the Hult Center for the Performing Arts when in Eugene, a cast of twenty principal, company, and aspirang dancers showcases a blend of classical and contemporary works in addition to offering a range of educational programs and services at home and on the road.

Eugene's contemporary, renegade ballet company, the elite troupe of dancers trained at Ballet Fantastique, strictly follow the Vaganova Method, a Russian-style technique and training system devised by the late dancer and master instructor Agrippina Vaganova. Like the Eugene Ballet Company, Ballet Fantastique headlines at the Hult Center for the Performing Arts; the upcoming season promises four performances, two new masterworks, bold live music, and dramatic storytelling.

1 Eugene Center
541-682-5000, hultcenter.org

Eugene Ballet Company: eugeneballet.org
Ballet Fantastique: balletfantastique.org

29

CELEBRATE THE HEART OF SUMMER
AT THE LANE COUNTY FAIR

A milestone mid-summer tradition in Eugene is the Lane County Fair. Running for five consecutive days during the third week of July, the fair draws families, teens, and adults to experience classic fair fun ranging from roller coasters and rides on the Ferris wheel to chances to win oversized stuffed animals from one of the carnival games on the midway. Fairgoers can expect pigs racing for Oreo cookies, musical entertainment with nightly headliners, food trucks, beer carts, local vendors, and exhibits and displays ranging from books to artwork, quilts, and photography. Not to be missed are the animal competitions for the Lane County Youth Fair, which are held in the livestock complex and arenas behind the main stage.

796 W Thirteenth Ave.
atthefair.com

Discounted season passes are available at Lane County Bi-Mart customer service counters for the two weeks leading up to the fair. Season passes are good for all five days and are ten dollars off face value when purchased at Bi-Mart stores. Different admission specials run each day; consult the Lane County Fair website for details.

30

GRAB BIG AIR
AT AN INDOOR GYMNASIUM OR TRAMPOLINE PARK

Indoor gymnasiums and trampoline parks are a parenting godsend on weekends, on no-school days, and throughout Oregon's rainy season. Eugene has three unique options: one favors trampolines, one specializes in recreational and competitive gymnastics, and one offers classes in the aerial arts. Each location offers different hours and prices; check the websites for complete details.

National Academy of Artistic Gymnastics (NAAG)
1205 Oak Patch Rd.
541-344-2002
naag-gymnastics.org

Bounce Gymnastics and Circus Arts Center
329 W Third Ave.
541-343-4222
bouncegymnastics.com

Get Air Eugene
4211 W Eleventh Ave.
541-827-1016
getaireugene.com

LAUGH
WITH THE SHORT ORDER KOOKS IMPROV TROUPE

Perfecting short-form improv for the past four years, the Short Order Kooks improvisational comedy troupe takes the stage at Sam Bond's Brewing Company the second Monday of every month (6:30 p.m. to 8:30 p.m.). Audience participation is encouraged as comedians play games ranging from the Dating Game to Alien Interview. Never tried improv but always wanted to give it a whirl? Join the group for bi-monthly practice/workshops at the McNail-Riley House on the first and fourth Monday of each month (7:00 p.m. to 9:00 p.m.).

Sam Bond's Brewing Co.
540 E Eighth Ave.
541-246-8162
sambondsbrewing.com

McNail-Riley House
601 W Thirteenth Ave.

WATCH AN INDIE FLICK
AT AN INDIE THEATER

Lovers of indie films, foreign, classic films; documentaries; retro-flashback parties; and second-run movie showings will love these three independently owned theaters within Eugene.

A stone's throw from the Fifth Street Public Market, the David Minor Theater and Pub encourages food and drinks inside its intimate two-screen theater. With traditional concessions, beer on tap, and a full wine menu, David Minor has partnered with two nearby restaurants and will place and deliver meal orders during the show. The theater provides small tables for anyone balancing a plate; couches at the front of theater one are popular with the date-night crowd.

A cornerstone business in the heart of the West Broadway shopping, dining, and entertainment district, Broadway Metro serves traditional and upscale concessions ranging from chocolate espresso beans to maple-walnut shortbread. Or pair a local beer, cider, or bottle of kombucha with your bag of popcorn.

Housed in a refurbished historic church, the Bijou Art Cinemas is the closest theater for students at the University of Oregon. Opened in October 1980, the Bijou has a long-standing reputation for bringing the finest foreign, independent, and classic films to town. As with the other theaters, expect wine, beer, and a variety of traditional and novel items on the concessions menu.

Bijou Art Cinemas
492 E Thirteenth Ave.
541-357-0375
bijou-cinemas.com

Broadway Metro
43 W Broadway
541-686-2458
broadwaymetro.com

David Minor Theater and Pub
180 E Fifth Ave.
541-762-1700
davidminortheater.com

TIP

All three theaters periodically offer "dinner and a date" or "two for one" discount ticket packages on Groupon.com.

SUPPORT INDEPENDENT COMMUNITY ACTORS

AT VERY LITTLE THEATRE

Founded at the onset of the Great Depression, Very Little Theatre has been a self-sustaining community theater since 1928. Located near the intersection of Hilyard Street and East Nineteenth Avenue, the theater's current venue features a 220-seat Mainstage Theater and Stage Left, a smaller and more intimate space for new directors and playwrights to showcase their skills. Playbills for five shows appear between the months of October and August, with ten to fourteen performances per show. Productions range from comedies to drama and musicals, with full descriptions, seats, and pricing listed on the theater website. Auditions are open to the general public, including individuals interested in backstage or technical roles.

2350 Hilyard St.
541-344-7751
thevlt.com

TRAVEL BACK IN TIME
WITH RADIO REDUX

Long-time Eugene resident Fred Crafts founded Radio Redux in 2009 with a vision of bringing back the Golden Age of Radio—an era of broadcasting that used live sound effects, handheld scripts, and in-studio musical performances to create informative and entertaining broadcasts for listeners seated in parlors across America. During the live show, members of the repertory theater company don retro 1940s attire and speak into vintage-style microphones. Audience members are advised to close their eyes and listen; performers may play more than one character (tip: follow the character, not the actor). Five shows run at the Hult Center for the Performing Arts between September and April, with discounts and preferential prices and registration dates offered to season ticket holders.

radioreduxusa.com

35

THINK OUTSIDE THE BOX
IN AN ESCAPE ROOM

The latest trend in adventure-game entertainment, escape rooms have been popping up in cities around the world for just over a decade. Inspired by "escape the room" style video games, physical escape room locations require teams of players to solve puzzles and riddles and search for hidden messages, with the objective of escaping the room within a set time limit. A challenging but rewarding teambuilding activity, escape rooms can be played alongside friends, family, co-workers, and strangers. To make the game more interesting, the rooms often have a unique theme, ranging from space stations to laboratories, carnivals, and even prison cells. Three local escape room locations, two in Eugene and one in Springfield, offer unique ways for guests to "think outside the box."

DARE Escape and Adventure Rooms
2160 W Eleventh Ave., Suite I
541-409-8894
dareescaperooms.com

Trapdoor Escape Rooms
436 Charnelton St.
541-937-5063
trapdooreugene.com

Escape the Room
303 S Fifth St., Suite 230, Springfield
541-726-3836
escapetheroomoregon.com

36

UPGRADE TO DINNER AND A SHOW

AT THE ACTORS CABARET

In good company among the many choices in Eugene's vibrant community theater scene, the Actors Cabaret of Eugene (ACE) has gained a reputation as the city's premiere dinner theater destination. It currently presents between six and eight productions per year, with more than 450 plays and musicals performed in front of hungry crowds throughout the organization's nearly forty-year history. Ticket options range from "dinner and a show" or "dessert and drinks" on Friday and Saturday evenings to "brunch and a show" during the Sunday matinee. Reserved seating is determined by type of ticket, with specific early arrival times for guests ordering a multi-course meal. Cast members are volunteer actors, musicians, and technicians of varying ages and backgrounds; many use their ACE experience to launch careers in drama and theater arts.

996 Willamette St.
541-683-4368
actorscabaret.org

BUILD PROJECTS AND FRIENDSHIPS
AT THE CRAFT HOUSE

Lane County's first DIY workshop space for women and corporate team-building events, the Craft House seeks to empower people one power tool at a time. It is located in a century-old refurbished church in the neighboring community of Goshen. Bolts of brightly colored fabric and spools of whimsical ribbon counterbalance an organized panel of drills, nail guns, and orbital sanders. Workshops are organized into two themes; crafting and building, with projects ranging from leather earrings to wooden plant stands. With an established presence in the local crafting community, the Craft House is as much a social club as it is a safe place to get creative and learn new skills. Projects vary each month; photos, measurements, and costs are listed on the Craft House website. (Materials, tools, and snacks are included in the cost of the workshops.)

85896 First St.
541-914-5990
thecrafthouseor.com

38

SPEND YOUR QUARTERS
AT A VIDEO ARCADE

In a city that thrives on counterculture, it's no surprise Eugene offers two sizeable arcades. Blairally Vintage Arcade is a destination attraction at the north end of Eugene's eclectic Whiteaker neighborhood. Drawing in both hippies and hipsters, Blairally is known for its variety of vintage arcade games, pinball, skee ball, and the old-school ball bowler machine. A popular family destination on Friday nights, Free Play Friday is open to minors until 9 p.m. Patrons order beverages and pub food from the bar and stay for the DJ or live music that runs until bar time. Closer to downtown (and just five blocks from the University of Oregon campus), Level Up Arcade blends classic games with modern favorites, ranging from multi-player games to shooters, drivers, air hockey, and even hoops-style basketball. Occupying an entire city block, Level Up offers lots of space to mingle, dance, and hang out with friends. As at Blairally, minors are welcome until 9 p.m., and patrons can order drinks and small bites and appetizers from an abbreviated menu. DJs, live music, themed parties, and weekly karaoke are regular entries on the Level Up event calendar.

Blairally Vintage Arcade
245 Blair Blvd.
541-683-1721

Level Up Arcade, 1290 Oak St.
541-654-5632
leveluparcade.com

39

WEAR A TOGA
TO *NATIONAL LAMPOON'S ANIMAL HOUSE* MOVIE FILMING SITES

One of the most iconic American film comedies of all time, *National Lampoon's Animal House,* was filmed in and around Eugene in the fall of 1977. The filmmakers needed a campus setting for the fictitious Faber College, and administrators at the University of Oregon gave Universal Studios permission to film at two fraternity houses located just off campus. While the derelict Delta Tau Chi fraternity was demolished in 1986, movie fans will recognize the white colonial columns of the Omega House/Phi Kappa Psi building at 729 East Eleventh Street. On campus, Hayward Field was the site of the golf scene, 110 Fenton Hall staged the courtroom scene, Gerlinger Hall was home to Emily Dickinson College, and the Erb Memorial Union fishbowl cafeteria withstood the epic food fight. Otis Day and the Knights performed "Shama Lama Ding Dong" at the Dexter Lake Club, a location under new ownership but with the original roadhouse allure. South of Eugene, the city of Cottage Grove closed down Main Street for three days while runaway floats and unguided marching bands wreaked havoc in the closing scenes.

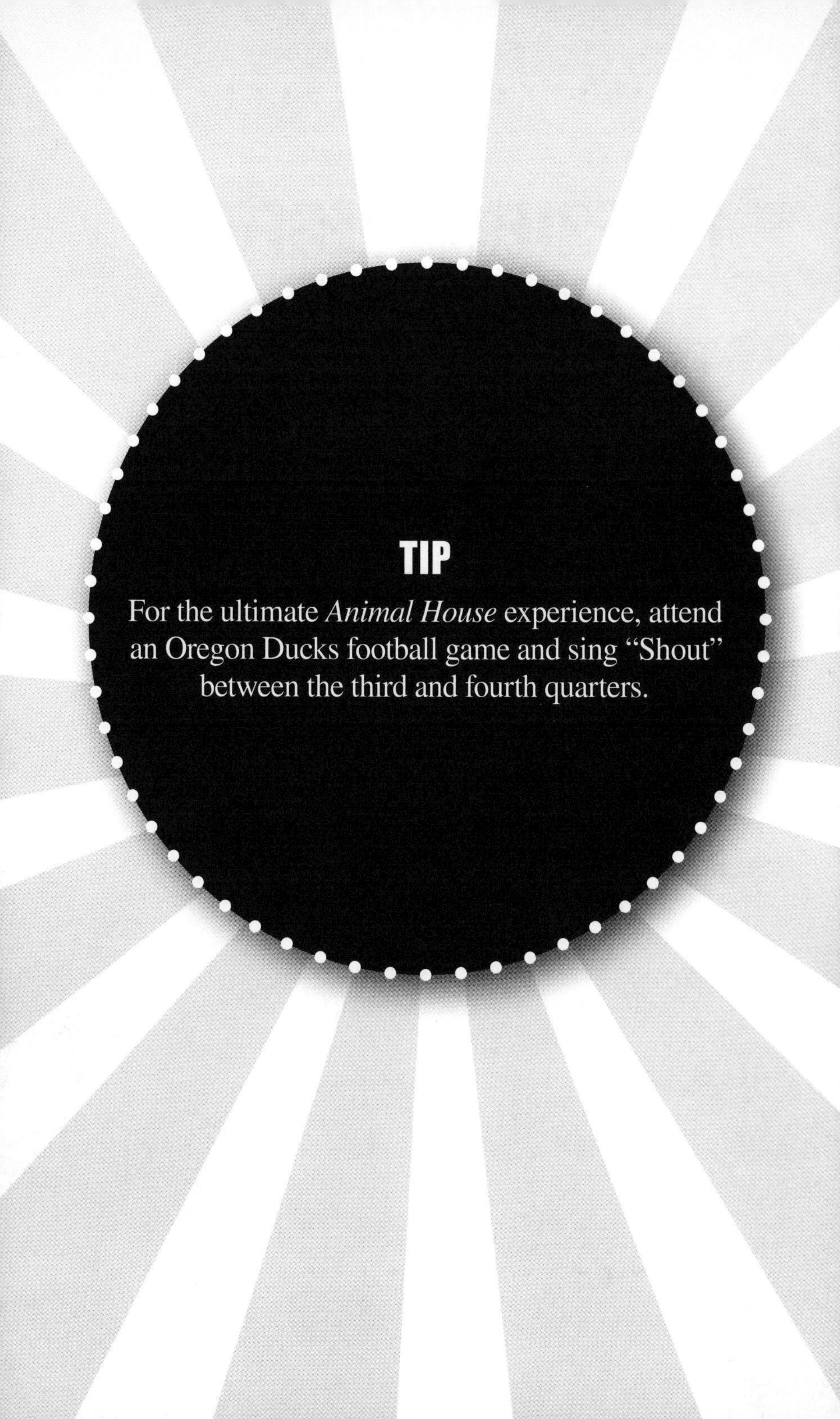

TIP

For the ultimate *Animal House* experience, attend an Oregon Ducks football game and sing “Shout” between the third and fourth quarters.

EXPERIENCE LEGENDS AND LEGACIES
AT THE OREGON BACH FESTIVAL

Produced by the University of Oregon, the Oregon Bach Festival is a sixteen-day celebration of chamber music, choral-orchestral composition, guest artists, educational programs, and social events. An annual event running in late June and early July, the Grammy Award-winning festival has been presenting the masterworks of J. S. Bach for nearly five decades. A broad range of music and events are scheduled at the historic Beall Concert Hall on the University of Oregon campus and the Silva Concert Hall and Soreng Theater at the Hult Center for the Performing Arts (with a handful of satellite events in Portland). It is designed to offer musical inspiration for everyone, and guests are invited to attend for just one day or come "Bach" for more.

975 E Eighteenth Ave.
541-346-5666
oregonbachfestival.com

41

PICK UP A PASSPORT

FOR EUGFUN! ALL SUMMER LONG

Always free. Always fun. All year long. EUGfun! is a calendar-based listing of ongoing community events sponsored by the city. Ranging from outdoor movies to pool parties; music, art, and theater events; and ice-cream socials, events are designed with the entire family in mind. Encompassed under the EUGfun! umbrella are Eugene Sunday Streets and Party in the Parks. Occurring twice each summer, Sunday Streets are well-attended events that promote healthy, active living by opening several miles of the city's largest public space—its streets—for people to experience and discover fitness activities such as dancing, yoga, walking, and biking. Similar to Sunday Streets, Party in the Parks feature active recreation, live music, and local food. Events run Tuesday evenings at neighborhood parks throughout the city.

eugene-or.gov/732/EUGFun

FOULS
PLAYER FOUL
SCORE
MATCH
5
02

SPORTS AND RECREATION

GO FOR A RUN
IN TRACK TOWN, USA

As you drive past the Eugene city limits, look for the green and white road signs that read "Welcome to Eugene. Pop. 157,100. Track Town U.S.A." Eugene is considered the birthplace of modern jogging and the catalyst for recreational running across the United States, and some days it seems like the entire city is out pounding the pavement.

To get your heart rate going, clock some miles on these popular running trails.

Pre's Trail at Alton Baker Park: A four-mile running and walking trail built in the fall of 1975 as a tribute to Steve Prefontaine.

Amazon Trail: A popular one-mile bark-chip loop located just south of the McChesney Memorial Track at South Eugene High School. It is marked every quarter mile, and an inner kilometer loop is marked every one hundred meters.

Rexius Trail: A three-and-a-half-mile cedar-chip trail along both sides of Amazon Creek in South Eugene. The Rexius Trail connects to the Amazon Trail at the halfway point and has mile markers every half mile.

Ruth Bascom Riverbank Path System: A network of twelve paved miles of interconnected mixed-use trails lining both sides of the Willamette River.

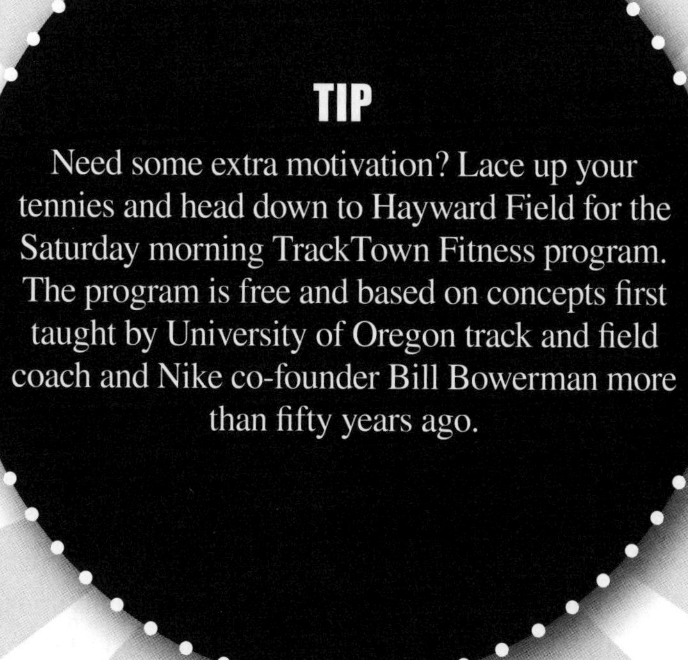

TIP

Need some extra motivation? Lace up your tennies and head down to Hayward Field for the Saturday morning TrackTown Fitness program. The program is free and based on concepts first taught by University of Oregon track and field coach and Nike co-founder Bill Bowerman more than fifty years ago.

43

BREAK OUT YOUR BINOCULARS
AT DELTA PONDS CITY PARK

A 150-acre waterway and city park, Delta Ponds is a favorite local destination for bird-watching; fishing; and hiking, biking, and jogging along a network of bike and pedestrian paths. It is relatively close to Valley River Center and a collection of chain stores, car dealers, office buildings, and apartment complexes. Keep an eye out for a small parking lot near the intersection of Goodpasture Island Road and Alexander Loop. An urban oasis of sorts, the park was recently restored with 2.2 miles of slow-moving side channels of the nearby Willamette River to provide areas of calm water during high-winter flows, ultimately improving the habitat for the juvenile spring Chinook salmon. Visitors enjoy just under a mile of gravel trails, bridges, viewpoints, and benches—keep an eye out for turtles, butterflies, birds, beavers, and river otters. Connector trails lead into and out of the Delta Ponds loop and connect to the Delta Ponds pedestrian bridge as well as the paved Ruth Bascom Riverbank Path System.

Goodpasture Island Road and Alexander Loop
eugene-or.gov/Facilities/Facility/Details/133

44

CHEER FOR THE JAMMERS
AT EMERALD CITY ROLLER DERBY

With origins dating back to the 1930s, and a resurgence in popularity around the turn of the twenty-first century, roller derby remains a female-dominated contact sport. It is played by two teams of five individuals roller-skating in the same direction around an oval track. Points are scored when designated "jammers" from each team lap members of the opposing team, all while the rest of the field is assisting and deflecting the field of players circling in the same direction. Bouts are fast paced and competitive and tremendously fun to watch; each player takes a pseudonym or "skate name," such as Purr Anna, Smother Theresa, or Bully Jean. Members of the Women's Flat Track Derby Association (WFTDA), Emerald City Roller Derby has been active in Eugene since 2006. Comprising the Emerald City Junior Gems, Emerald City All Stars, Wizards of Quad, and Team Emerald, teams compete regionally and internationally. Lane County Concussion is the only local men's roller derby team. Tournaments and bouts are typically held at the Lane Events Center at the Lane County Fairgrounds campus in Eugene or the Bob Keefer Center for Sports and Recreation in Springfield. Check the event calendar published on the ECRD website for times, dates, and other important details.

Bob Keefer Center, 250 S Thirty-Second St., Springfield

Lane Events Center, 796 W Thirteenth Ave.
ecrg.com

DANCE THE HOKEY POKEY
AT SPRINGFIELD SKATE WORLD

The disco balls at Springfield Skate World have been spinning over the indoor roller-skating rink since the mid-1970s—a venue where locker rentals are still a quarter and the hustle dance move never went out of style. A popular destination for birthday parties, first dates, and family traditions, Skate World has recently gotten a small face-lift, including six hundred new pairs of rental skates and new menu items, such as pizza, at the concession stand. As you might expect, a DJ "spins" tunes from an elevated corner booth and coordinates rink games, such as the hokey pokey and the giant dice game. Arcade games frame the rink for any non-skaters or skaters taking a bit of a break.

3188 Gateway Loop, Springfield
541-746-8424
skateskateworld.com

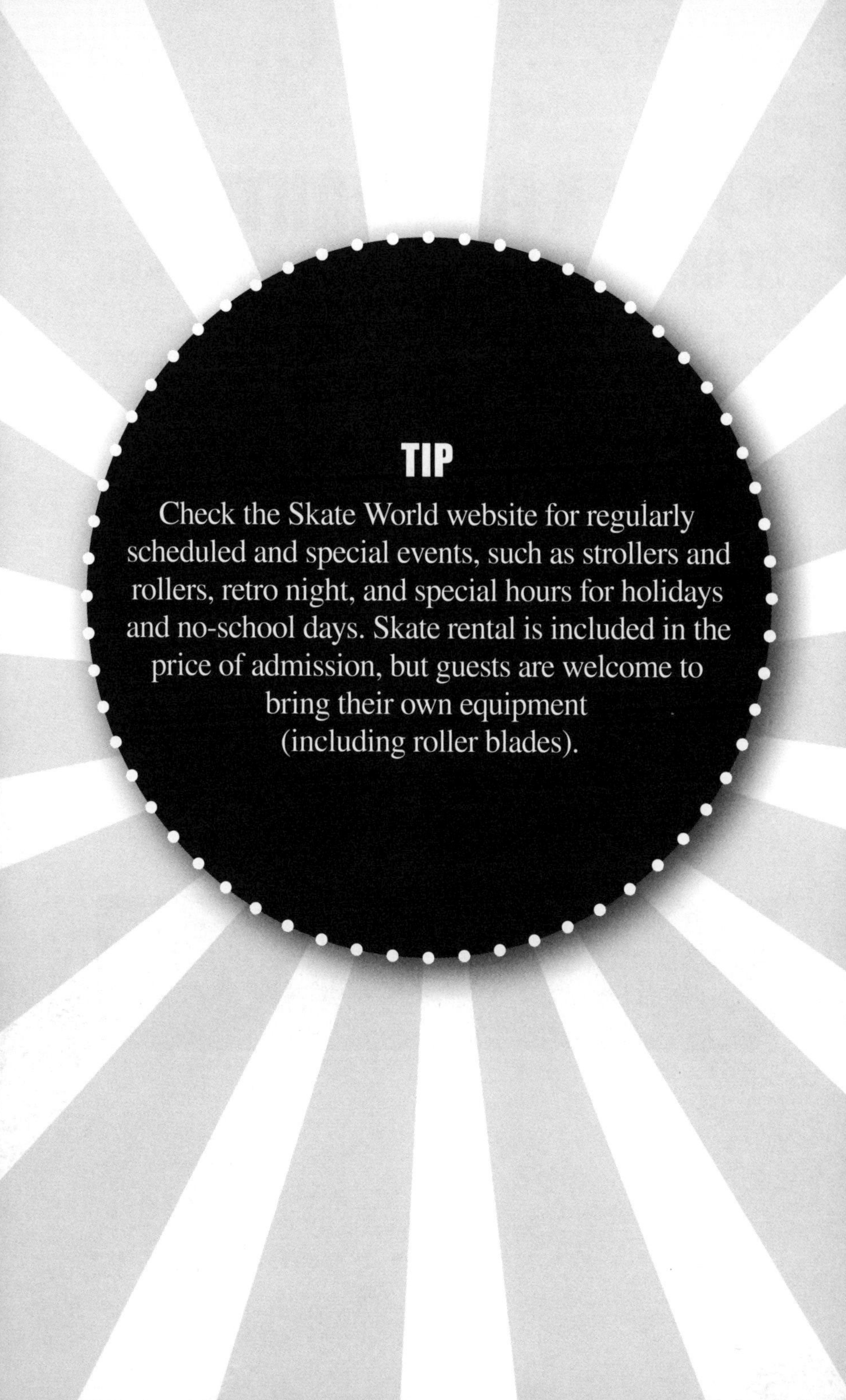
TIP
Check the Skate World website for regularly scheduled and special events, such as strollers and rollers, retro night, and special hours for holidays and no-school days. Skate rental is included in the price of admission, but guests are welcome to bring their own equipment (including roller blades).

PLAY A FULL EIGHTEEN
AT CAMP PUTT ADVENTURE GOLF PARK

Yet another family-friendly venue maintained by the Willamalane Park and Recreation District, Camp Putt Adventure Golf Park in Springfield offers two eighteen-hole miniature golf courses—both with water elements and an even mix of easy and challenging holes. An outdoor attraction, Camp Putt is open seasonally, with more weekend hours in the spring and fall and daily (10 a.m. to 9 p.m.) once school is out for the summer. Camp Putt Adventure Golf Park shares a parking lot with Roaring Rapids Pizza Company. If you visit during golf season, the two venues are easily combined for a half-day (or more) outing.

4006 Franklin Blvd., Springfield
541-852-4653
willamalane.org/facility/camp-putt

TIP

Hang onto your scorecard to use the two-for-one admission coupon for your next golf outing.

ROOT FOR THE REDS
IN SUPPORT OF LANE UNITED

From flag-wavers and drumbeaters to pint raisers and face painters, fans show up in red in support of the Lane United Football Club. One of seventy amateur soccer teams in the Premier Development League (PDL), Lane United travels across Oregon, Washington, and British Columbia for away games. Supported by the Red Aces (aka the Lane United Supporters Trust), beer and gear sales at home games help offset player expenses, purchase new equipment, and cover travel expenses on the road. Home games draw fans to the main field at the Bob Keefer Center in Springfield. Games are about as family friendly as they come; players walk onto the field with kids from local teams, and you may stand for the US and Canadian national anthems. Common chants are published on the Red Aces website and sung to the tune of familiar tunes ranging from "Glory Glory Hallelujah" to Billy Joel's "Piano Man."

250 S Thirty-Second St., Springfield
laneunitedfc.com
red-aces.org

48

TAKE SOMEONE OUT TO THE OL' BALLGAME

AT PK PARK

Craving some peanuts and Cracker Jack? Take your family out to the ol' ballgame all summer long at PK Park, a four-thousand-seat, $19.2 million state-of-the-art stadium and home field for the Eugene Emeralds. Members of the Northwest League, the "Ems" are currently Class A short season affiliates of the Chicago Cubs. As with minor league games across America, a night at PK Park is more about making family memories than tracking RBIs. Between innings lucky fans compete in zany games on the field, spectators answer trivia questions on the digital scoreboard, and occupants of randomly selected blocks of seats win goodies like free pizza and gear. If the Ems strike out the opposing team's designated beer batter, the over-twenty-one crowd receives discounted craft beer for a short period of time (when the heckling begins, make a beeline for the beer tent). Younger fans may prefer Sluggo FunZone; look for the bounce house and inflatable obstacle course behind the bleachers down the left field line. Located behind the University of Oregon's Autzen Stadium, the venue offers ample and easy parking all season long.

2760 Martin Luther King Jr. Blvd.
541-342-5367
emeraldsbaseball.com

49

WATCH FOR THE SLAP SHOT

AT THE RINK EXCHANGE

Yet another reason to visit the Lane County Fairgrounds campus is the Rink Exchange, Eugene's lone venue for figure skating and hockey. For the past twelve seasons, the Rink Exchange has served as home ice for the Eugene Generals, a United States Premier Hockey League Tier III Junior A hockey team. Games are fast paced and family friendly, with the level of competition and rivalry one would expect at a semi-professional athletic event. When the Generals are off the rink, the facility is a popular destination for open skating, skating lessons, hockey practice, and even birthday parties.

796 W Thirteenth Ave.
541-225-5123
therinkexchange.com

TIP

Don't have your own skates? Rent a pair for three dollars from the pro shop during public skate hours.

GET THE KIDS
TO RIVERPLAY DISCOVERY VILLAGE PLAYGROUND

A community project spearheaded by the Eugene Rotary Club, the RiverPlay Discovery Village Playground introduces kids to the unique elements of Eugene's history and culture. The multi-element complex is contained within a one-acre expanse of land between Eugene and Mary Skinner's original one-room pioneer log cabin and the paved Ruth Bascom Riverbank Path System. Imagination is encouraged as kids play in a Kalapuya summer dwelling, ride in a stage coach, dig for dinosaur fossils, or climb on a replica of the basalt rock columns that tower over Skinner Butte Park in real life. In warmer weather, the Rain Circle structure feeds into the headwaters of the Willamette River; water play elements are activated at the push of a button between the hours of 9 a.m. and 8:30 p.m. (a towel or change of clothes might be a good idea here). Drinking fountains, indoor restrooms, picnic tables, benches, and nearby parking are available RiverPlay Discovery Village.

248 Cheshire Ave.
www.eugene-or.gov/Facilities/Facility/Details/45

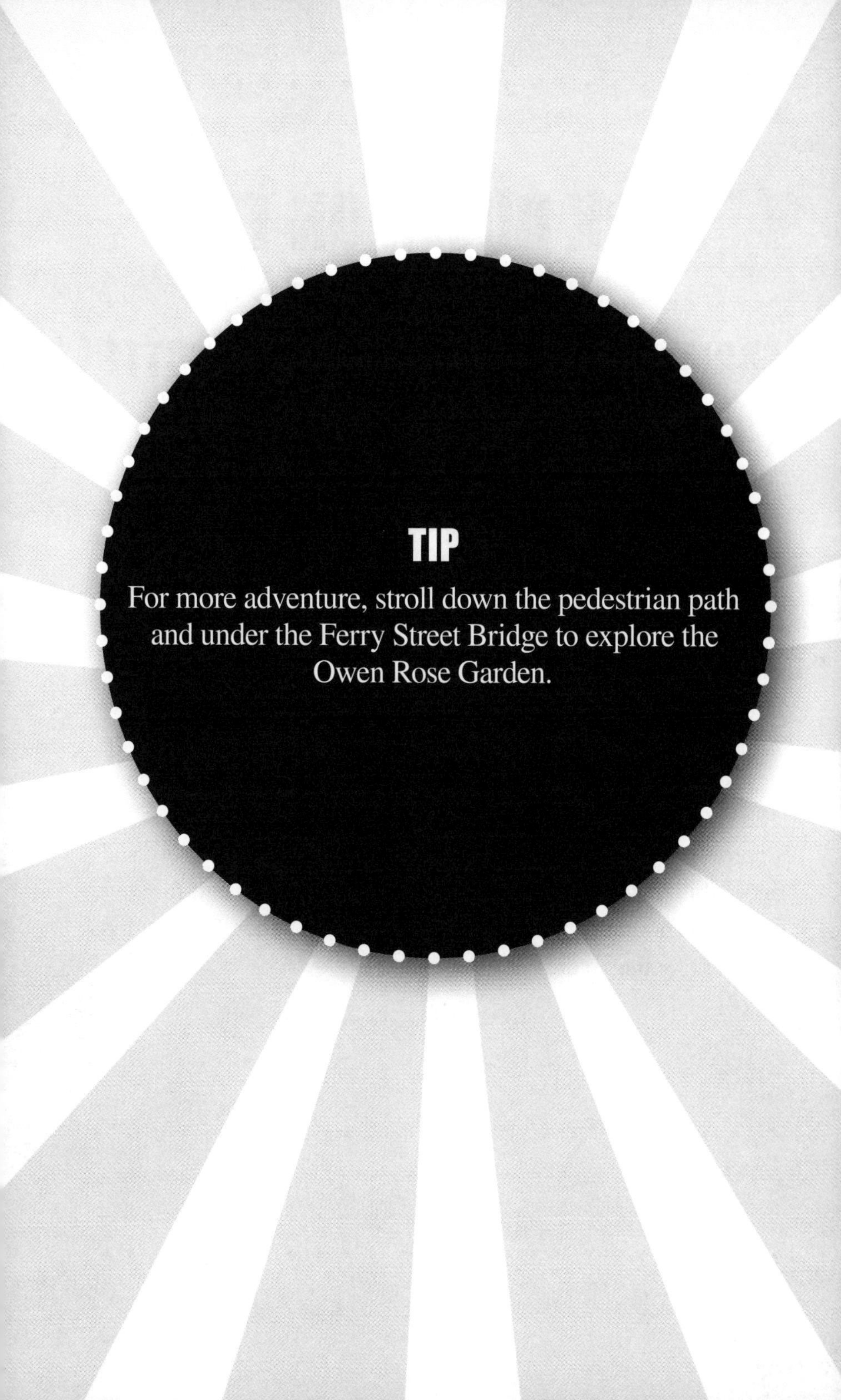
TIP
For more adventure, stroll down the pedestrian path and under the Ferry Street Bridge to explore the Owen Rose Garden.

51

LOOK DOWN ON THE EMERALD VALLEY

FROM THE SUMMIT OF SPENCER BUTTE

At an elevation of 2,058, Spencer Butte is the tallest and most prominent landmark in the Southern Willamette Valley. The city's highest point, Spencer Butte is contained within the Ridgeline Trail System, a series of large, public parklands connected by a network of more than twelve miles of trails and seven main trailheads. Visitors who park at the Spencer Butte trailhead will hike just more than one mile the summit, with a total elevation gain of 784 feet. It is considered a moderate to difficult hike. A verdant canopy of dense ferns and majestic Douglas firs gives way to a rocky outcropping as the summit comes into view. Within the last year, more than 120 basalt steps have been added to the trail's final ascent, an improvement that both combats erosion and improves safety and accessibility. Make sure to bring a camera, as the reward for your effort is panoramic views of the entire Emerald Valley. Expect mud and slick footing in the rainy season.

85385 S Willamette St.

TIP

Spencer Butte is a popular hike; parking may be challenging in nice weather and on the weekend. Remember to use the portable toilets at the trailhead and carry water if you need it.

GO BIG OR GO HOME
AT ALTON BAKER PARK

Weighing in at 413 acres, Alton Baker Park holds bragging rites as Eugene's largest city park. Named after Alton F. Baker, Sr., the founder of the *Register-Guard* daily newspaper, the Alton Baker is roughly half the size of New York's Central Park. You'll need several trips to experience dozens of unique attractions within West Alton Baker Park and the Whilamut Natural Area, highlights including: Steve Prefontaine's running trail (Pre's Trail); the Cuthbert Amphitheater, the Science Factory Children's Museum and Planetarium; Hays Tree Garden; a BMX track; a disc golf course; a dog park; sports fields; picnic shelters; and hourly canoe, kayak, and paddleboard rentals through Northwest Canoe Tour. Connected to downtown Eugene by the Ferry Street pedestrian bridge, Alton Baker Park hugs the north bank of the Willamette River under Interstate 5 in the direction of Springfield. Partially contained within the park, and starting with the sun near the water garden, are the planets in a 1:1 billion scale model of the Solar System. It ends with Pluto, 3.7 miles away near the Randy Pape Beltline overpass on the Ruth Bascom Riverbank Path System.

100 Day Island Rd.
541-682-4800
eugene-or.gov/altonbakerpark

CLIMB THE WARPED WALL
AT THE NORTHWEST NINJA PARK

One of Springfield's newest and coolest attractions is Northwest Ninja Park, a five-thousand-square-foot indoor training facility that features some of the most iconic obstacles from the hit television show *American Ninja Warrior.* Founded by show participant hopeful Sloane Cameron, the park focuses on building agility, balance, strength, and endurance through obstacle training. Obstacles range from the ultimate cliffhanger to adult and youth warped walls, double salmon ladders, pegboards, floating doors, aerial silks, and a cannonball alley. Already drawing interest from participants of all ages and abilities, Northwest Ninja Park offers classes and open gym time for enthusiasts age four and up.

873 Shelley St., Springfield
541-600-8224
nwninjapark.com

TIP

Attention parents, Northwest Ninja Park offers two-hour birthday party packages for groups of up to fifteen kids.

ATTEND WALK THE LAND DAY AT GREEN ISLAND

Formed by the confluence of the McKenzie and Willamette rivers, Green Island is a one-thousand-acre open space located just west of downtown Coburg. The largest piece of property protected under the umbrella of the McKenzie River Trust, a nonprofit land trust formed to protect critical habitat and scenic lands in the McKenzie River basin, Green Island is open to the general public only one day each year as part of Walk the Land Day, a statewide day of events at places protected by land trusts. Activities at Green Island Walk the Land Day range from bird walks to fishing, tractor rides, mountain biking, and conservation tours. With opportunities for solitude, the event also pulls in local entertainment and a row of conservation and education booths from local sponsors, as well as the Oregon Department of Fish and Wildlife. Picnicking is encouraged; the event is both free and fun for the entire family. Access to Green Island outside of Walk the Land Day is restricted to volunteer projects and group tours (see the McKenzie River Trust website for dates and details).

mckenzieriver.org

FLOAT DOWN THE ALTON BAKER CANAL

WITH NORTHWEST CANOE TOUR

Looking for something new to float your boat? Why not head down to Alton Baker Park and rent a canoe, kayak, or stand-up paddleboard from Northwest Canoe Tour? A convenient way to get onto the water without having to haul any equipment, Northwest Canoe Tour provides instruction, life jackets, and general guidance on navigating the park's two-mile canoe channel (essentially a side channel of the Willamette River). Rentals run on a first-come-first-served basis between 11 a.m. and 5 p.m. on Fridays, Saturdays, Sundays, and holidays. Alternatively, the outfitter's designated Tuesday Tours take participants out onto lakes and rivers in a group setting. Tuesday Tours run forty dollars per person and include a guide, orientation, outfitting, paddling, lunch, and a discussion about local natural history.

222 Day Island Rd.
541-579-8990
canoetour.org

56

JOIN A HUMAN FOOSBALL LEAGUE
WITH PLAYGROUND SPORTS

A new take on a classic arcade game, human foosball transforms teams of six to ten adults into real-life game pieces. It is a fast-paced and high-energy sport, but the way to win remains the same—kick, bounce, and bump a ball into the opposing team's net. The challenge? Players must maintain contact with the PVC poles and can move side to side, but no spinning is allowed. Managed by Playground Sports—a popular local recreational sports league that caters to the adults' inner child—human foosball is played on a portable thirty-eight-foot long by fourteen-foot wide oval court. Leagues currently run between October and May at Oakshire Brewing at 1055 Madera Street. Friendly competition and friendlier camaraderie are encouraged; alcoholic beverages are not permitted near the field of play (however, a plethora of options await thirsty players in the taproom).

1055 Madera St.
541-221-2392
playgroundsports.com

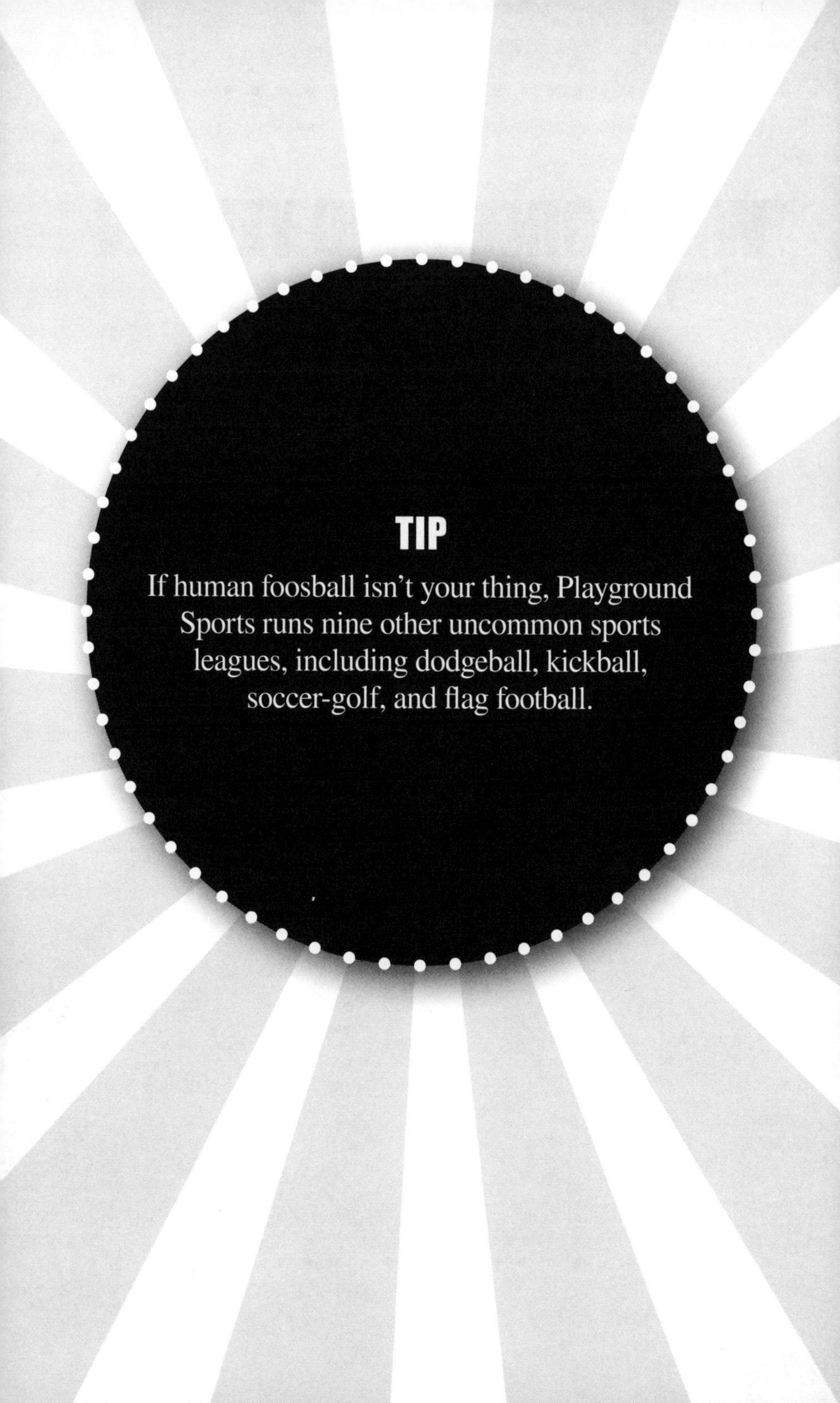

TIP

If human foosball isn’t your thing, Playground Sports runs nine other uncommon sports leagues, including dodgeball, kickball, soccer-golf, and flag football.

57

WEAR GREEN AND YELLOW
TO A DUCKS FOOTBALL GAME

A university town in every way, Eugene is fiercely loyal to the University of Oregon and Oregon Ducks football. Come the first part of September, citizens from near and far break out their best yellow and green gear and head to Autzen Stadium to tailgate before every home game. It is a family-friendly affair that spans generations, and fans come together to grill burgers, toss beanbags, and socialize. Before the game, the marching band winds through the parking lot to fire up the crowd before heading into the stadium for some NCAA Division 1, Pac-12 Conference action. Unique game day traditions include motorcycles escorting the team onto the field, the Duck mascot dropping for pushups for every point added to the scoreboard, and the entire stadium singing and dancing to Otis Day and the Knights' version of "Shout" between the third and fourth quarters.

2700 Martin Luther King Jr. Blvd.
goducks.com

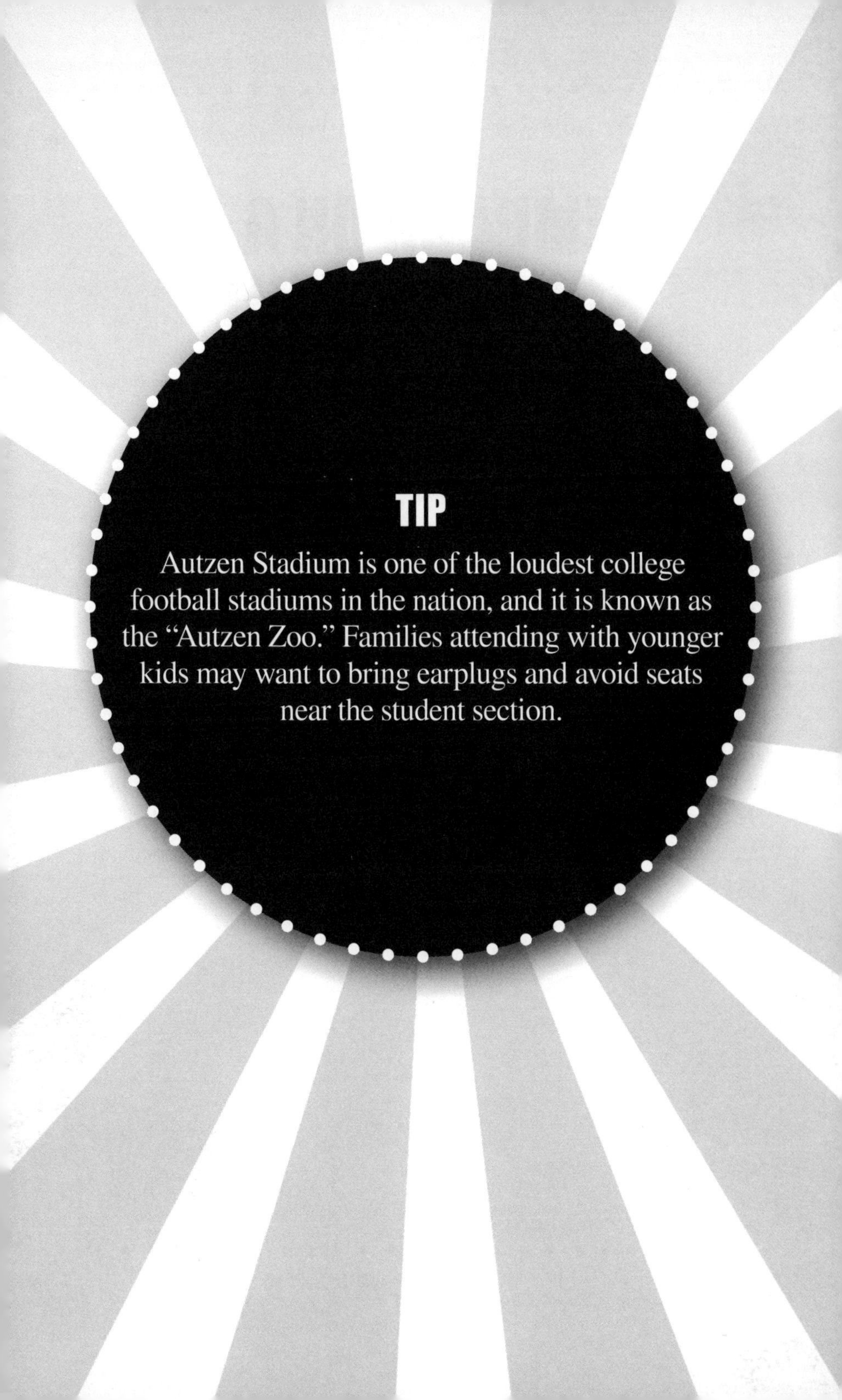

TIP

Autzen Stadium is one of the loudest college football stadiums in the nation, and it is known as the "Autzen Zoo." Families attending with younger kids may want to bring earplugs and avoid seats near the student section.

EMBARK ON A SUNDAY STROLL

AT FERN RIDGE RESERVOIR

With thirty miles of shoreline wrapping around a ten-thousand-acre body of water, Fern Ridge Reservoir ranks among the largest bodies of water in Lane County. Located on the Long Tom River approximately fifteen miles west of Eugene, the reservoir is a popular place for hiking, biking, swimming, camping, picnicking, boating, fishing, and birding. A near constant breeze and five-mile expanse of water running north to south contribute to the lake's popularity with wind surfers and sailors; water depth averages eleven feet and is maintained by a flood control dam at the mouth of the river. While approximately 85 percent of the reservoir lands are open to the general public, common gathering spots are Perkins Peninsula Park, Zumwalt Park, Orchard Point Park, and Richardson Park.

GO AHEAD AND SPLASH!
AT LIVELY PARK

Located on the far eastern edge of Springfield, Splash! at Lively Park is worth the drive if you have kids. An indoor attraction open year round and maintained by the Willamalane Park and Recreation District, Splash! features a large wave pool, lap pool, adults-only hot tub, kiddie pool, and twisty water slide. Lively Park is also the site of a fantastic outdoor playground structure (on par with the RiverPlay Discovery Village Playground in Eugene), dog park, and covered picnic shelters.

6100 Thurston Rd., Springfield
541-736-4244
willamalane.org/facility/splash-at-lively-park

TIP

Look for a two-dollar-off family admission coupon to the pool in one of the local savings books delivered to your mailboxes every month, and don't forget to start a frequent swimmer punch pass.

60

FLOAT IN SALT WATER
AT TAMARACK AQUATIC CENTER

At ninety-two degrees, the saltwater of the therapeutic swimming pool at Tamarack Aquatic Center offers a range of health benefits, from increased mobility to relief for sore muscles and joints. Frequented by citizens of all ages, Tamarack Aquatic Center is a place for socialization, swimming lessons, and a range of aquatic wellness programs. Open year-round, the pool is a delightful distraction on a cold and rainy winter day. Hours and prices vary but include drop-in rates and discounted punch cards. A destination attraction within the Tamarack Wellness Center, Tamarack Aquatic Center shares its location with a collection of independent healing arts practitioners and Eugene Yoga. Take a minute to walk the campus and get inspired to heal your mind, body, and soul.

3575 Donald St.
541-686-9290
tamarackwellness.com

FIND YOUR FAVORITE ROUTE

AT CRUX ROCK CLIMBING GYM

Designed with the outdoor climber in mind, the walls and routes at Crux Rock Climbing Gym include arêtes, roofs, overhangs, low angles, and bouldering caves. With thirty rope stations (eighteen leadable) throughout the nine-thousand-square-foot facility, Crux is a popular destination year-round, particularly during the wet and rainy season. Equipment rental and lessons are available; routes are changed regularly for all skill levels.

401 W Third Ave.
541-484-9535
cruxrock.com

TIP

When you're ready to practice outside, make the short journey to Skinner Butte Park for the fifty-foot-high basalt rock columns featuring bolted anchor points, multiple cracks, and more than fifty routes for beginners and experienced climbers.

RENT A PRIVATE HOT TUB OR SAUNA
AT ONSEN SPAS

Nestled between Franklin Boulevard and the Willamette River on Garden Avenue is a relaxing sanctuary—hourly hot tub and sauna rentals at Onsen Spas. Seeking to provide guests with the many health and wellness benefits of traditional Japanese spa practices, Onsen features a row of private open-air rooms that run both sides down a quiet brick-and-cedar-lined corridor. Open year-round and seven days a week, Onsen Spas is a particular cold-weather favorite. Reservations are suggested and available no less than one hour and no more than twenty-four hours in advance. Rates vary based on group size, guest age, and rental package.

1883 Garden Ave.
541-345-9048
onsenspas.com

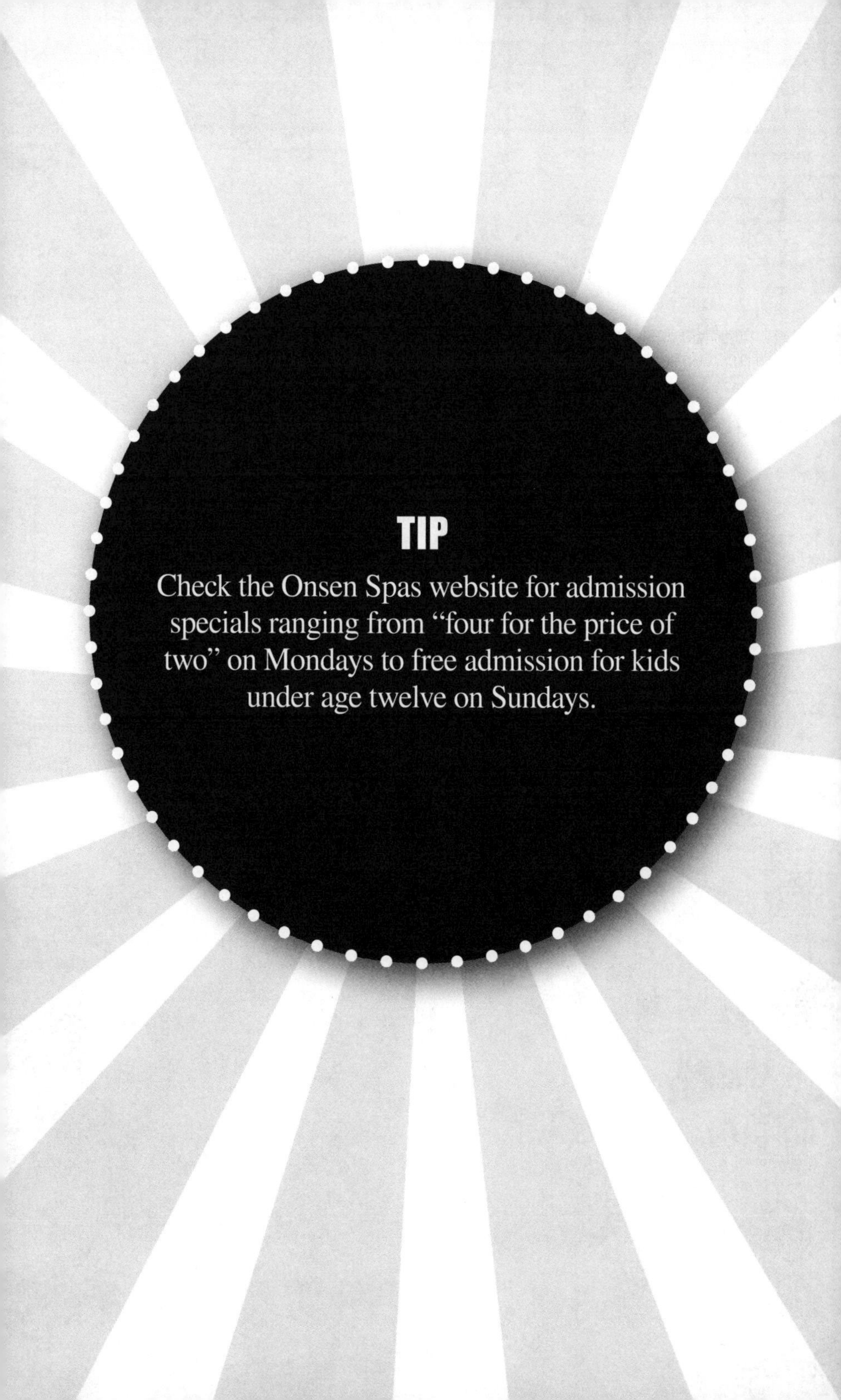

TIP

Check the Onsen Spas website for admission specials ranging from "four for the price of two" on Mondays to free admission for kids under age twelve on Sundays.

CULTURE AND HISTORY

APPRECIATE ALL FORMS OF ART
DURING FIRST FRIDAY ARTWALK

On the first Friday of every month for the past forty years, downtown Eugene has placed a special emphasis on the arts. From pop-up galleries to musical performances in public places and artists specializing in various forms, First Friday ArtWalk pays tribute to its vibrant and talented community. It is overseen by the Lane Arts Council, and more than thirty galleries, studios, shops, and restaurants regularly participate with free guided tours beginning at 5:30 p.m. Tours lead participants through five of the featured venues, with artist interviews (ArtTalks) and open forum discussions about the project and the medium. Many destinations offer special discounts and incentives for frequenting their location during ArtWalk. A similar venue on a smaller scale, downtown Springfield hosts a Second Friday Art Walk on—you guessed it—the second Friday of each month.

Downtown Eugene
lanearts.org/first-friday-artwalk

64

FOLLOW THE PROGRESS
OF THE 20X21EUG MURAL PROJECT

Third in global reach and magnitude, behind the Olympic Games and the FIFA World Cup, is the International Association of Athletics Federations (IAAF) World Championships. Hosted bi-annually in notable destinations around the world, the event draws packed stadiums and television audiences in the billions. Slated for the 2021 games, the city of Eugene has launched a public art program that celebrates the diversity and cultures represented at the games. To date, twenty artists of varying backgrounds and training have been commissioned to install unique public artwork by the year 2021. It is aptly named the 20X21EUG Mural Project. Details on the project, artists, and installation schedules are available on the City of Eugene website.

eugene-or.gov/3492/20x21-EUG-Mural-Project

LEARN ABOUT HAZELNUTS AND LOCAL HISTORY AT DORRIS RANCH

A national historic site, a working farm, and a public park, Springfield's Dorris Ranch takes several hours to fully explore. It is the oldest commercial hazelnut (filbert) farm in continuous operation in America, and more than seven hundred thousand pounds of nuts are harvested each year. Dorris Ranch is a popular destination for school groups during the week and wedding parties on the weekend. Guests meander through seventy-five acres of hazelnut trees or in the direction of the Living History Village, with its pioneer-era buildings, farm tools, and Native American plank house. A recent addition to the park property is a paved, four-mile path that runs between Dorris Ranch and Clearwater Park along the middle fork of the Willamette River.

205 Dorris St., Springfield
willamalane.org/park/dorris-ranch

66

EMBARK ON A SELF-GUIDED TOUR

OF THE HISTORIC FARMERS' UNION MARKETPLACE

Occupying the full city block running between West Fifth Avenue and West Sixth Avenue and Olive and Charnelton streets are the historic remains of what was once the Farmers' Union Cooperative /Pacific Cooperative collection of buildings. It was once a hub of agricultural commerce, and farmers came to the cooperatives to buy and sell feed, seed, and eggs. Listed on the National Register of Historic Places, today's Farmers' Union Marketplace is a collection of retail businesses contained within two buildings. Inside Down to Earth Home, Garden, and Gift is a self-guided walking tour of the Farmers' Union building, including original machinery, wood floors, grain bins, hoppers, and chutes; pick up a copy of the tour pamphlet from the cashier station and look for marked placards within the store's interior. Alternatively, worth investigating is the extensive photovoltaic solar panel system generating renewable energy on the roof of the Pacific Cooperative building (look for equipment and signage inside the Allann Brothers coffee shop).

532 Olive St.
541-342-6820
downtoearthhomeandgarden.com

67

STOP AND SMELL THE ROSES
AT OWEN ROSE GARDEN

Portland may claim bragging rights as the City of Roses, but Eugene offers a slice of olfactory heaven at Owen Rose Garden. Eugene's second-oldest public park, Owen Rose Garden received its name after lumberman George Owen donated it to the city in 1951. Located just west of the Washington-Jefferson Street Bridge, this 8.5-acre city park features more than 4,500 roses in more than four hundred varieties—requiring a fleet of volunteers for ongoing and strategic planting, mulching, fertilizing, and pruning. To find this olfactory sanctuary, enter through the small parking lot at the end of Jefferson Street or meander in from the pedestrian path that runs along the Willamette River. Accessible pathways frame manicured lawns as they travel around ornate gardens, under verdant arbors, and into a twenty-eight-foot covered gazebo popular with the wedding scene.

300 N Jefferson St.
eugene-or.gov/facilities/Facility/Details/124

EDUCATE YOURSELF
AT THE LANE COUNTY HISTORY MUSEUM

Housed within the Lane County Fairgrounds campus, the Lane County History Museum tells the story of Lane County. Seven permanent exhibits feature artifacts, photographs, and documents dating back to the time of covered-wagon immigration. Life-size replicas range from the original 1853 Lane County clerk's building to a miniature blacksmith forge. Smaller displays showcase household items, medical kits, books, and maps. Traveling exhibits rotate through the facility, with information and dates listed on the "Current Exhibits" section of the museum website. It is a two-story museum, but the bulk of the visitor experience is distributed throughout the first floor. History buffs and genealogists may get more out of this venue; ask for a scavenger hunt sheet on a clipboard as a way to keep younger kids engaged. You'll also find a trunk of period clothing and puppet theater near the staircase leading to the second floor.

740 W Thirteenth Ave.
541-682-4242
lchm.org

GIVE A HOOT
ABOUT THE CASCADES RAPTOR CENTER

The Cascades Raptor Center is a non-profit nature center and wildlife hospital dedicated to rescue, rehabilitation, and release of raptors native to the Pacific Northwest. Some of the birds are permanent residents, and some are on medical leave, so to speak. Others may go out to local schools with center staff. It is open six days per week, and visitors to the center meander the trails around the lower and upper aviaries. Getting to the Cascades Raptor Center is an adventure in itself; the facility sits on the back side of Spencer Butte. If the parking lot is full, take care when leaving your vehicle on Fox Hollow Road. The majority of the raptor experience is outside, and you'll want to dress for the weather. Visitors pay a general admission fee but can upgrade to an annual membership if they're feeling philanthropic after a visit.

32275 Fox Hollow Rd.
541-485-1320
cascadesraptorcenter.org

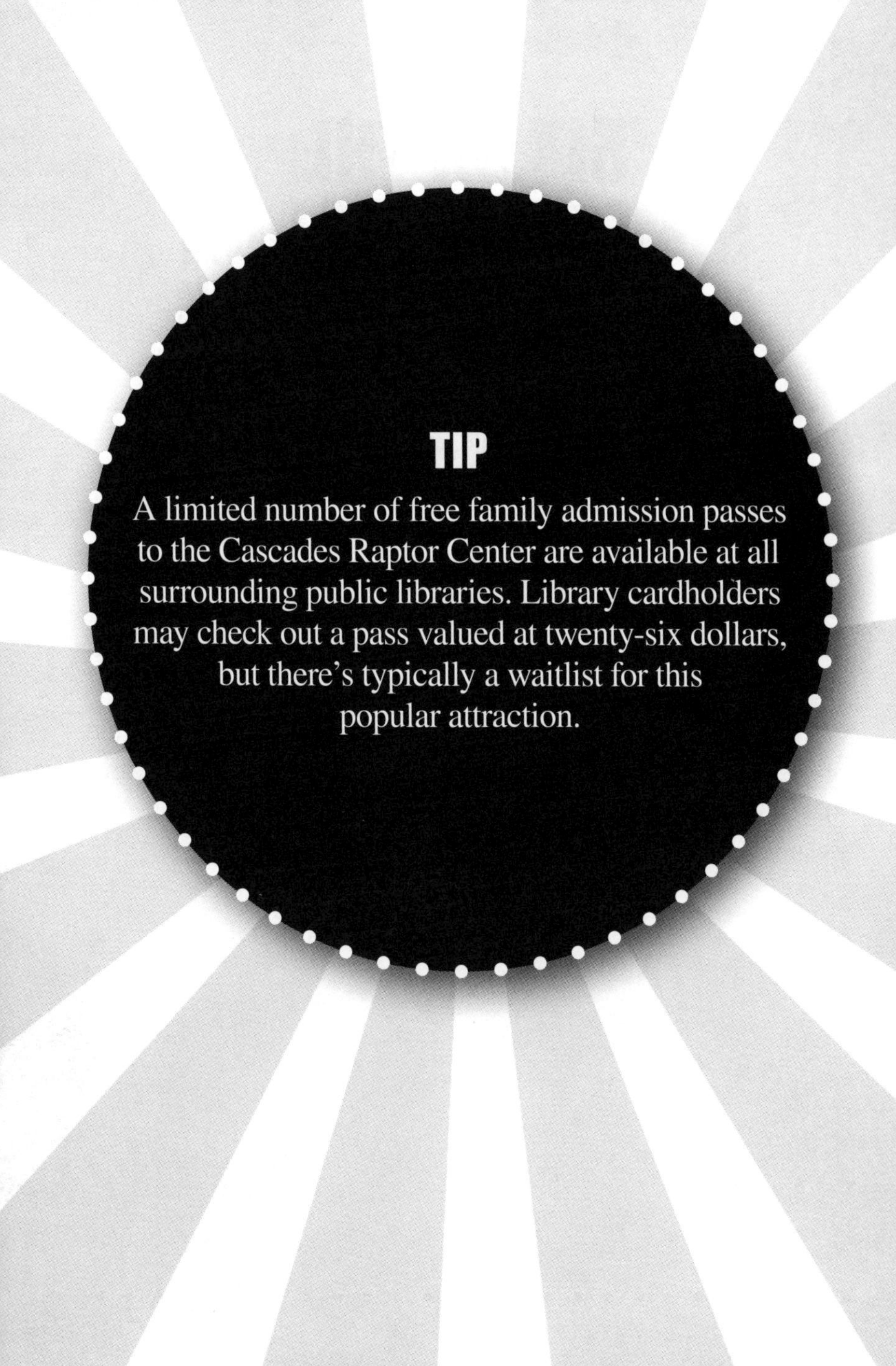

TIP

A limited number of free family admission passes to the Cascades Raptor Center are available at all surrounding public libraries. Library cardholders may check out a pass valued at twenty-six dollars, but there's typically a waitlist for this popular attraction.

SIT ON THE SIMPSONS' COUCH

AT THE SPRINGFIELD MUSEUM

The stately brick building that now houses the Springfield Museum once held three three-story transformers used by the Oregon Power Company to provide the city with electricity. Free and open to the general public Wednesday through Saturday, the museum highlights the history of Springfield and the surrounding area, with an emphasis on the influence of the lumber, industrial, and agricultural industries. The bulk of the permanent collections is located on the second floor and ranges from a pioneer-era schoolhouse with toys and costumes to the Simpsons' Couch, a popular spot for a souvenir photo. Leave an hour to explore both floors, with extra time to view the documentary-style film and the historic and artistic exhibits that rotate monthly in the Kathleen Jensen Galllery.

590 Main St., Springfield
541-726-3677
springfield-museum.com

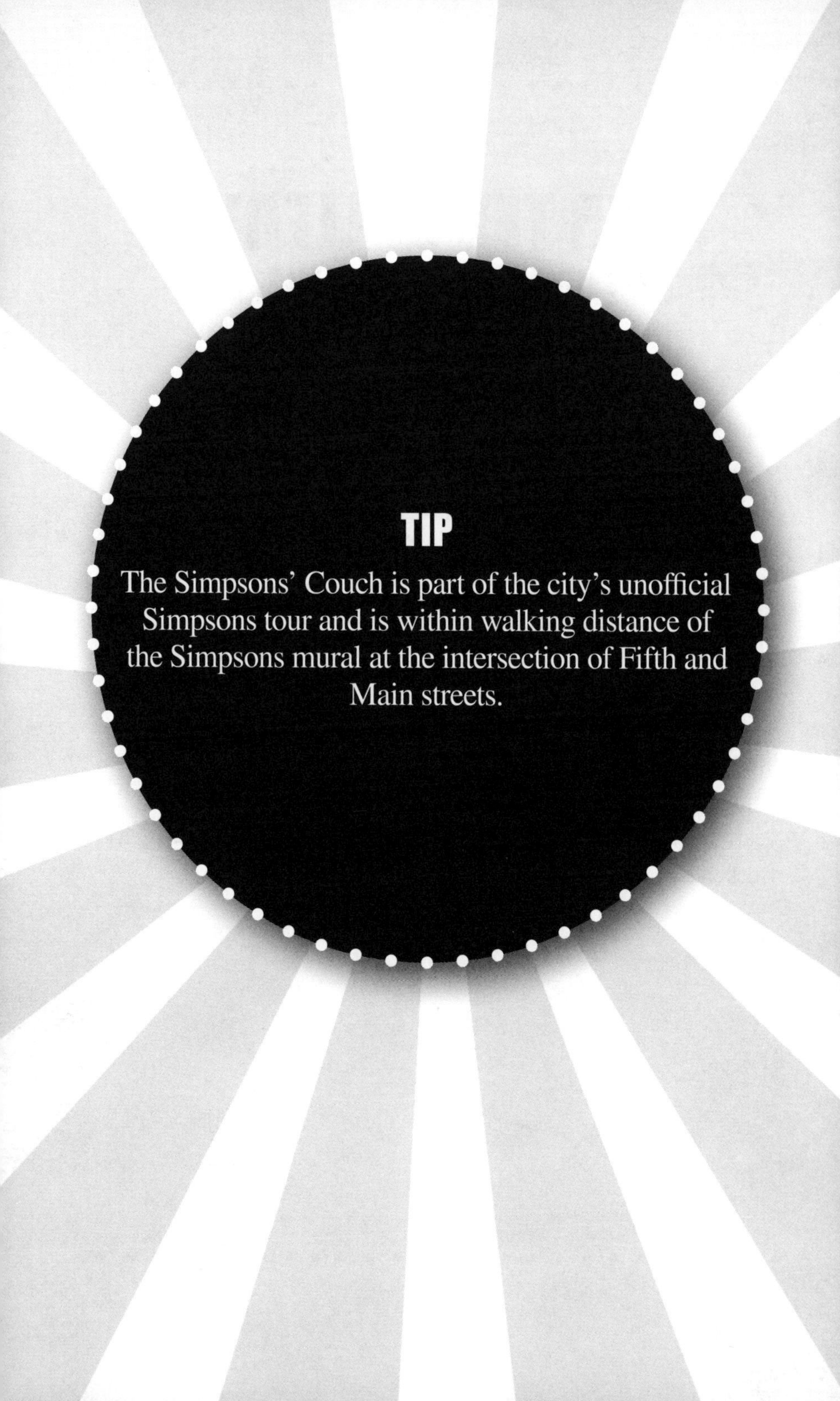

TIP

The Simpsons' Couch is part of the city's unofficial Simpsons tour and is within walking distance of the Simpsons mural at the intersection of Fifth and Main streets.

71

TOUR TEN GALLERIES
AT THE JORDAN SCHNITZER MUSEUM OF ART

Outdoor sculptures lead the way to the Jordan Schnitzer Museum of Art (JSMA), a hub of culture and creativity in the heart of the University of Oregon's sprawling campus. Although more than thirteen thousand works are displayed in ten galleries on a rotating basis, JSMA is perhaps best known for its extensive collection of Asian art. Museum exploration is self-guided or with the assistance of a cellphone-based audio program. Families with younger kids should inquire about the ArtPacks: multi-sensory activity kits available at the front desk that are designed to create a more interactive and age-appropriate educational experience. Lectures, workshops, demonstrations, and symposia occur throughout the year, with free admission for everyone on home football game weekends.

1430 Johnson Ln.
541-346-3027
jsma.uoregon.edu

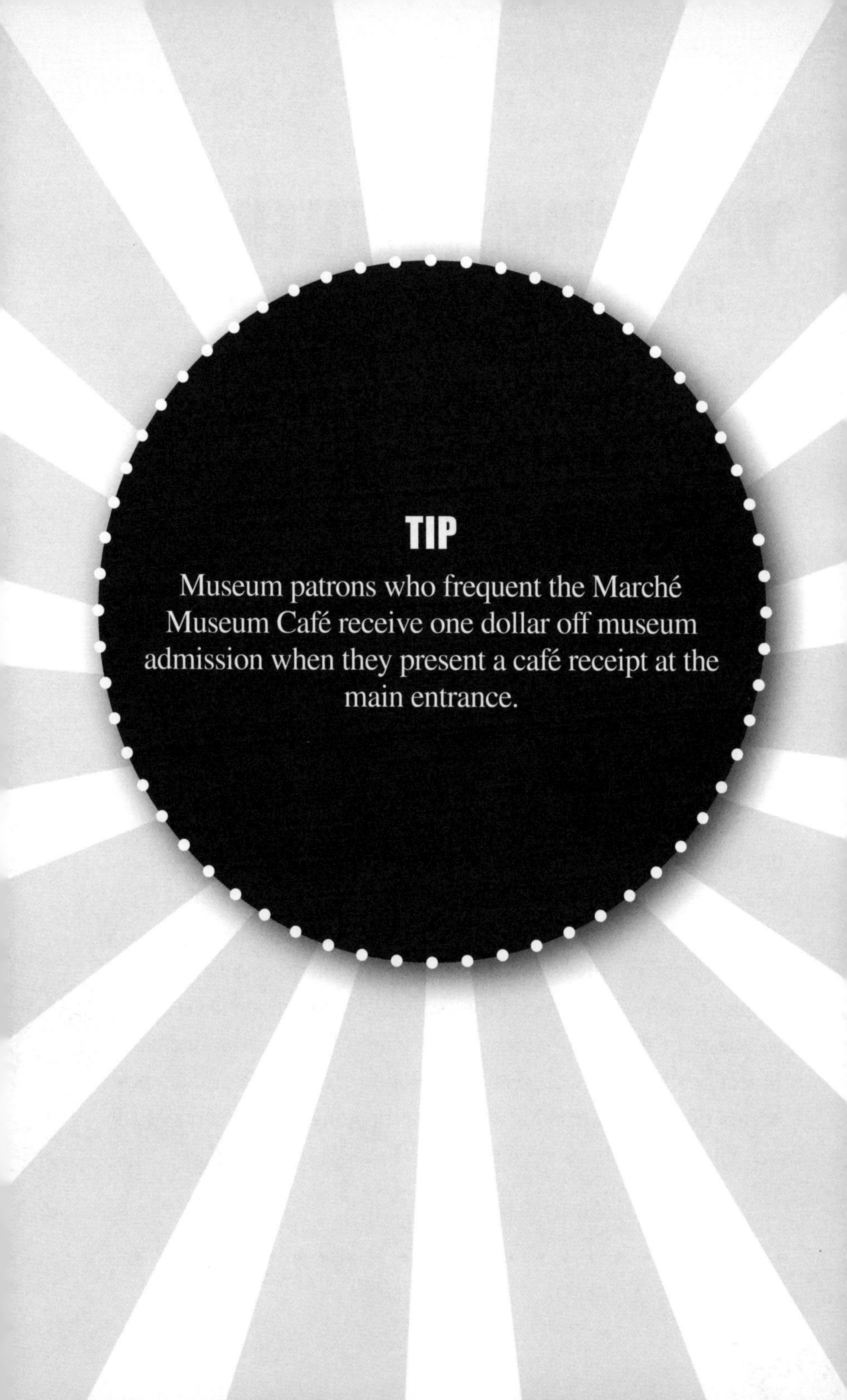
TIP
Museum patrons who frequent the Marché Museum Café receive one dollar off museum admission when they present a café receipt at the main entrance.

VIEW DOWNTOWN EUGENE
FROM THE "CASTLE ON THE HILL"

A notable Eugene landmark since 1888, the Shelton McMurphey Johnson House is the city's only Victorian house museum. Open to the public and available to rent for special occasions, the house features period furniture, photographs, and artifacts that preserve a century's worth of cultural evolution—from the lifestyle of the early pioneers through two world wars, including the addition of modern-day conveniences such as indoor plumbing and electricity. Owned by the city and overseen by the Shelton McMurphey Johnson Advisory Board, the majestic "Castle on the Hill" has been authentically preserved in its original location on the side of Skinner Butte overlooking the downtown business district and the Amtrak depot. The visitor experience is typically self-guided; visitors learn about the Shelton, McMurphey, and Johnson families through pamphlets and other museum literature. Volunteer docents answer questions and offer supplemental information about specific points of interest. Tour highlights include the family bedrooms, second-floor sleeping porch, attic, and turret, where Mr. Johnson spent much time in isolation. Approximately eight times throughout a year, afternoon tea is served to guests in the main parlor. Often paired with holiday including Valentine's Day, Mother's Day, and Holiday Teas in December, these events double as a fundraiser for the ongoing preservation of the building. Reservations are required.

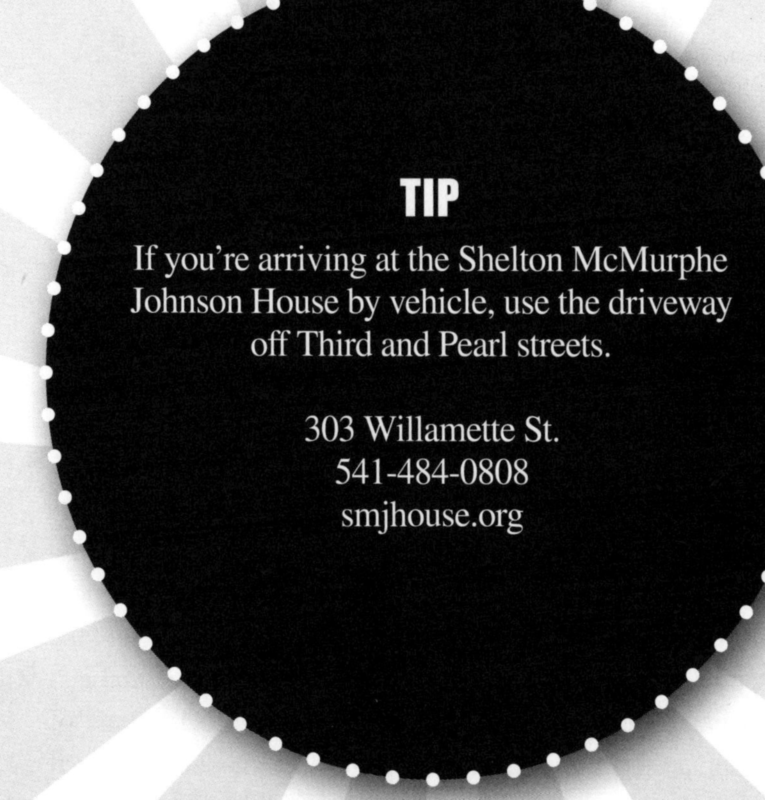

TIP

If you're arriving at the Shelton McMurphe Johnson House by vehicle, use the driveway off Third and Pearl streets.

303 Willamette St.
541-484-0808
smjhouse.org

73

ELEVATE YOUR DAY
AT THE OREGON AIR AND SPACE MUSEUM

Located just south of the Eugene Airport, the Oregon Air and Space Museum (OASM) is perhaps one of the best-kept secrets in town. The visitor experience is split between two large rooms, with the main hangar housing aircraft ranging from a replica of the world's smallest jet to scale models of SBD dive-bombers used in WWII. Guests then pass through a short outdoor corridor to a second hangar packed with large engines, smaller space artifacts, and even a row of jump seats. Many of the exhibits in this room are interactive, such as the cross-section display of the pistons and crankshafts necessary to propel a jet into the air. If you have the time, and a docent is available, a guided tour of the museum will give you a deeper understanding of global aviation history, the evolution of the commercial airline industry, and the back story on influential and instrumental aviators in Eugene and greater Oregon. The bulk of the aircraft, artifacts, uniforms, photos, and scale models have been donated to the museum or are on permanent display, a side note interesting in itself (be sure to read the placards about the donor or the donor's family).

90377 Boeing Dr.
541-461-1101
oasmuseum.com

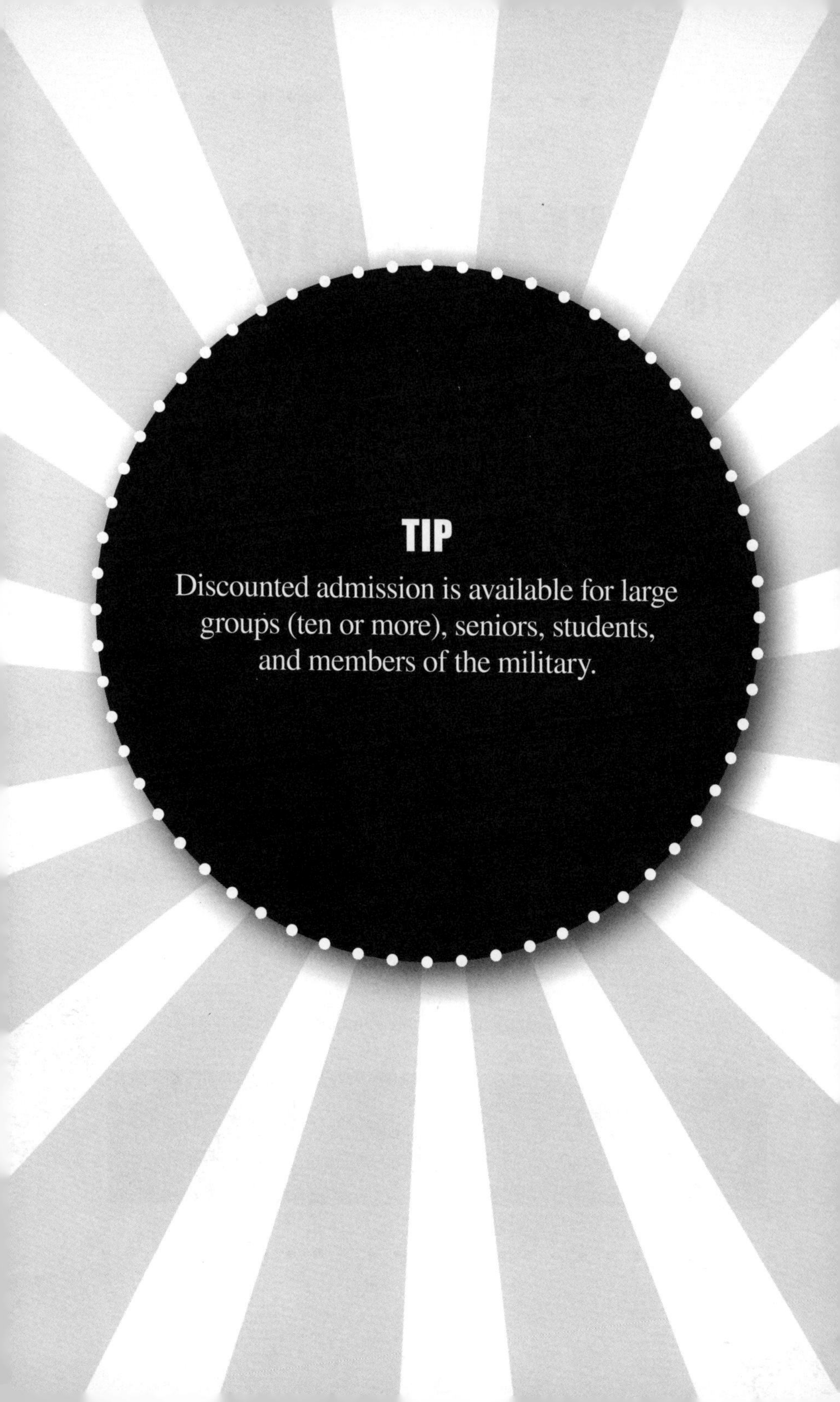
TIP
Discounted admission is available for large groups (ten or more), seniors, students, and members of the military.

74

TAKE A FIELD TRIP

TO THE MUSEUM OF NATURAL AND CULTURAL HISTORY

With a reputation as the premier natural and cultural history museum in the state of Oregon, the Museum of Natural and Cultural History is the largest natural history museum between Seattle and San Francisco. A center for archaeological and paleontological research, the facility is located in the heart of the University of Oregon and within walking distance of the Jordan Schnitzer Museum of Art. A popular school field trip destination, the Museum of Natural and Cultural History generally appeals to anyone interested in the natural history, geology, and archaeology of Oregon and the Pacific Northwest. Many of the exhibits are hands-on and range from fourteen thousand years of Native American tribal history and Oregon's changing landscapes, climate, and ecosystems to the surprising answers to when and how people first arrived in North America.

1680 E Fifteenth Ave.
541-346-3024
natural-history.uoregon.edu

TIP

General admission to the Museum of Natural and Cultural History is free on the first Friday of every month.

GO EXPLORING
AT THE ADVENTURE! CHILDREN'S MUSEUM

A place of joy and happiness, Adventure! Children's Museum is now open in a 2,500-square-foot interim space on the second floor of the Valley River Center shopping center (follow the giggles to the top of the escalator). The result of two years of fund-raising and grant writing, the museum is now a safe place for local children to learn, build, and use their imaginations. Themed around adventure and ethe notion that every child is an explorer, current exhibits are designed for children ages two to twelve and range from a tree house library to an art room, a Pacific Northwest camping corner, and Shakespeare's Globe Theater. This is considered an "incubator" location, so expect Adventure! Children's Museum to grow and expand in the coming years; future exhibits and whimsical interior design additions are listed on the museum website. And the best part for parents? General admission is only four dollars per person, with free admission for babies under age one. (Annual membership passports offer discounts on gift shop purchases and birthday party packages and come with an invitation to participate on the museum's advisory committee and vote in membership elections.)

490 Valley River Center
541-653-9629
adventurechildrensmuseum.org

STROLL THROUGH THE GARDENS
AT HENDRICKS PARK

Established in 1906, Hendricks Park is the oldest city park in Eugene. Less than a mile from the University of Oregon campus, the park is nestled in a seventy-eight-acre patch of urban forest between the historic Fairmont and Laurel Hill neighborhoods. Two designated garden areas draw visitors year-round, but especially in the peak of springtime blooms: the fifteen-acre established Rhododendron Garden and the newer five-acre Native Plant Garden. Wheelchair-accessible trails meander through the garden areas, with a network of packed dirt hiking trails (including an entry point into the Ridgeline Trail System) through the remainder of the property. Park visitors have access to water, modern restrooms, picnic pavilions, and picnic tables; dogs are permitted but must remain on a leash. Located nearby, the Pre's Rock memorial site is a short drive from the park's north entrance and just off Skyline Drive.

Summit Avenue and Skyline Boulevard
friendsofhendrickspark.org

REAP THE HARVEST
AT COMMON GROUND GARDEN

Occupying what was once a vacant lot in the heart of the Friendly Street neighborhood, the Common Ground Garden took the community garden philosophy and opened the grounds to everyone. Maintained by neighborhood volunteers and family-friendly work parties the first two Saturdays of every month, the garden's philosophy is simple: come in and pick what you need and want. A teaching farm as much as a social gathering place, Common Ground Garden offers opportunities to learn about seed saving, composting, permaculture, and gardening best practices. A viable and sustainable model for other neighborhoods to replicate, Common Ground Garden may just plant the seeds of change.

Twenty-First and Van Buren streets

GEEK OUT
AT THE SCIENCE FACTORY CHILDREN'S MUSEUM AND PLANETARIUM

Lane County's only hands-on science museum and planetarium, the Science Factory was originally founded as a branch of the Portland-based Oregon Museum of Science and Industry. It is housed in a brightly colored building in the heart of Alton Baker Park. Expect to spend a few hours working your way through the permanent and traveling exhibits explaining the science behind anything from magnetic poles to wind velocity. Visitors pay admission to just the museum or the planetarium, or receive a slightly discounted rate if purchasing both. Planetarium shows change every Wednesday at 3 p.m., with ongoing seasonal stargazing shows on Saturday and Sunday. This is a popular elementary school field trip destination. Check the museum website for a list of regular programs, summer camps, and special events.

2300 Leo Harris Pkwy.
541-682-7888
sciencefactory.org

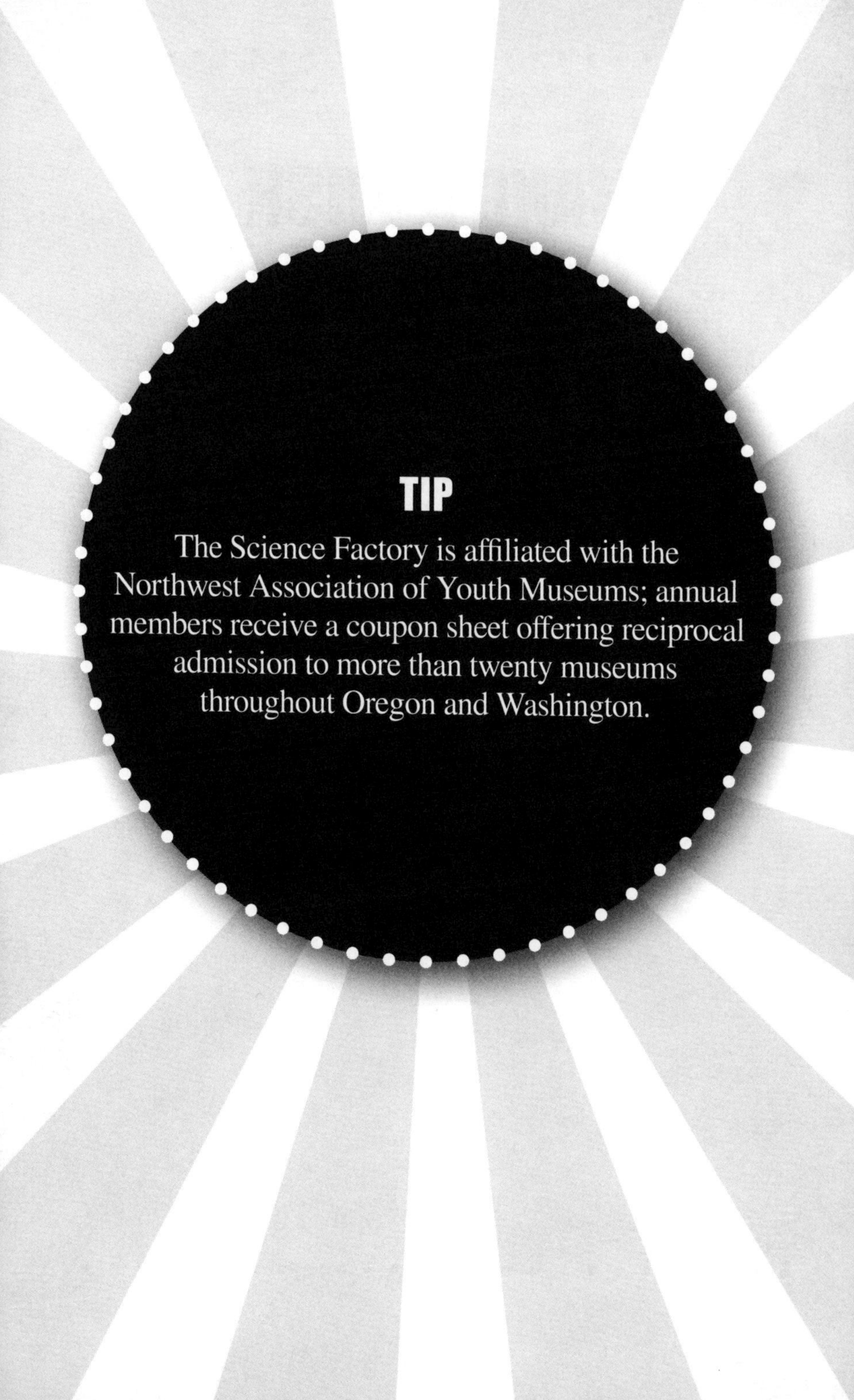
TIP
The Science Factory is affiliated with the Northwest Association of Youth Museums; annual members receive a coupon sheet offering reciprocal admission to more than twenty museums throughout Oregon and Washington.

HANG A WISH
ON EUGENE'S WISHING TREE

Supposed to have the power to fulfill wishes through nature, religion, or spirituality, wishing trees are portals for inner desires and longings. Located on the southeast corner of West Twentieth Avenue and Lincoln Street near Washington Park is Eugene's own wishing tree. To add a wish among the foliage, select a paper hangtag from inside the black metal mailbox located at the base of a large drooping ninebark (*Physocarpus*) shrubbery.

Southeast corner of West Twentieth Avenue and Lincoln Street

GO FOR A HIKE
ON THE RIDGELINE TRAIL SYSTEM

Equally popular among hikers, dog walkers, trail runners, and single-track mountain bikers is the Ridgeline Trail System, an extensive twelve-mile network of trails in South Eugene. Ridgeline trails run through Suzanne Arlie Park, Amazon Headwaters, Mt. Baldy, Blanton Ridge, Moon Mountain, South Eugene Meadows ,and Wild Iris Ridge and showcase Eugene's diversity in flora and fauna. Spencer Butte, the city's highest point, crowns the Ridgeline at 2,058 feet in elevation. While numerous paths lead into the main trails (many of which link residents to their neighborhoods), Ridgeline has seven main trailheads with designated parking and trail maps.

eugene-or.gov/Facilities/Facility/Details/129

TIP

Download a PDF map of the Ridgeline Trail System from the city of Eugene website or pick up a paper copy at the Travel Lane County: Eugene, Cascades, and Coast Visitor Center.

PLAY CAPTURE THE FLAG
AT PAINTBALL PALACE

A popular destination among Eugene's teenage crowd, Paintball Palace facilitates private events, such as company outings and adult birthday parties. It is the only indoor arena in town, paintballers over age ten are welcome to bring their own equipment or rent guns and safety gear from the pro shop. Teams start from opposite sides of the arena, seeking shelter in towers, behind metal tubing, and in semi-enclosed rooms. Staff members change the rules of the game, from attack and defend to capture the flag and protect the president. Not interested in paintball? Paintball Palace also houses an indoor black-light laser tag arena/glow-in-the-dark maze. Open play for paintball and laser tag starts at 2 p.m. each day; check the website for coupons off admission and equipment purchases.

1820 W Seventh Ave.
541-465-4766
paintballpalace-or.com

TIP

When playing paintball, dress in layers and wear old clothes. Gloves are also recommended for protecting bare hands.

PARTICIPATE IN A WALK OR WORKSHOP
AT THE MOUNT PISGAH ARBORETUM

A 209-acre living tree museum five miles outside of downtown Eugene, the Mount Pisgah Arboretum draws hikers, picnickers, school groups, and brides and grooms. Encompassed within the 2,363-acre Howard Buford Recreation Area (the largest of Lane County's seventy-three parks), the arboretum is named after Mount Pisgah—a summit 1,531 feet above sea level. A hike equal in popularity with Spencer Butte, a network of trails leads to the summit and offers options for different ways up and down the mountain. The Arboretum is open year-round, and staff schedule public "Walks and Workshops" events that range from birding to yoga, plant identification, art, and photography. Two annual events, however, draw the most visitors to the park: the Wildflower and Music Festival in May and the Mushroom Festival in October.

34901 Frank Parrish Rd.
541-747-3817
mountpisgaharboretum.com

TIP

Although there is no admission fee to visit Mt. Pisgah Arboretum, Lane County Parks charges a four-dollar daily parking fee.

83

PHOTOGRAPH EUGENE
FROM THE SUMMIT OF SKINNER BUTTE

Towering over the north edge of downtown Eugene, Skinner Butte is a prominent landmark that can be seen for miles around. It is a popular location for panoramic views of the downtown business district, residential neighborhoods, university buildings, and the Willamette River, and visitors have the option of driving or hiking to the summit. If arriving by vehicle, follow the signs to the summit from the basalt rock columns near the intersection of Lincoln Street and Skinner Butte Loop, or turn right onto Skinner Butte Loop from the parking lot of the Shelton McMurphey Johnson House. A network of hiking trails leads up to the summit. Park near the RiverPlay Discovery Village Playground or at the smaller lot at the base of the basalt rock columns. Noteworthy souvenir photography points are near the veterans' memorial flag at the center of the main summit parking lot and at the concrete twenty-by-thirty-foot letter O (representing the University of Oregon) slightly down the slope of the hill facing the city.

skinnersbutte.com

WATCH
THE CROWNING OF THE CITY'S NEW SLUG QUEEN

The unofficial goodwill ambassador of the city of Eugene is the SLUG queen (short for the Society for the Legitimization of the Ubiquitous Gastropod). A new queen is crowned the second Friday evening each August in a celebration of eccentric and eclectic pageantry—a true epitome of Eugene's hippie counterculture and a statement for wit and audacity over beauty and perfection. A tradition dating back to 1983, SLUG Queen duties have included presiding over the parade at the annual Eugene Celebration*, delivering a benediction at the Maude Kerns Art Center Jell-O Show, and holding a charitable ball for the charity of his or her choosing. SLUG Queens retain their title for life and are referred to as "old" instead of "former"—a popular SLUG Queen motto is "once a queen, always a queen."

slugqueen.com

*Dormant for the past few years, the Eugene Celebration parade was officially replaced by the inaugural 2017 EUG Parade—a new tradition that combines the best of Eugene Sunday Streets with the best of the Eugene Celebration.

STRIKE A POSE WITH THE SIMPSONS MURAL
IN SPRINGFIELD

The real Springfield is considered to be the inspiration for the fictional town of Springfield in the long-running animated television comedy *The Simpsons*, and the Simpsons mural pays tribute to Matt Groening and the many similarities between fiction and reality. Located on the west wall of the Emerald Art Center near the intersection of Fifth and Main streets in downtown Springfield, the fifteen-by-thirty-foot full-color installation is one of the most visited attractions in the city. A collaborative project between print artist Julius Preite and Groening himself, the Simpsons mural blends an iconic Oregon backdrop with the antics of Homer, Marge, Lisa, Bart, and Maggie. Building on the television-themed notoriety, the city of Springfield has organized an unofficial Simpsons tour with key stops at the Springfield Horseman Statue, Moe's Tavern, the Springfield Museum, and the Pioneer Statue at the University of Oregon.

Intersection of Fifth and Main streets, Downtown Springfield
eugenecascadescoast.org/simpsons/tour

86

JOIN THE TOOLBOX PROJECT

AND BUILD SOMETHING NEW

A tool lending library serving the many families and neighborhoods across Eugene and Springfield, the ToolBox Project offers low-cost access to building and garden tools for home and garden improvement projects. There's an annual membership price tag of twenty dollars per individual (or thirty dollars per household), and items ranging from hammers to power tools may be borrowed for one week. It is based out of a blue shed in the parking lot behind the Friendly Street Church, and open hours are Saturdays from 9 a.m. to 12 p.m. and Thursdays from 5 p.m. to 7 p.m. Opportunities to learn from others, use new equipment, and volunteer for community-centered work parties run throughout the year, with the ToolBox Project website and Facebook page the best sources of information.

2235 Adams St.
eugenetoolboxproject.org

ATTEND THE ANNUAL JELL-O SHOW

AT THE MAUDE KERNS ART CENTER

Housed in a refurbished nineteenth-century Presbyterian church in Eugene's historic Fairmont neighborhood, the Maude Kerns Art Center is the city's only non-profit community center for the visual arts. It offers classes, lectures, workshops, and summer camps, and guests are welcome to visit the center's gallery space when exhibits are on display (admission is free, and exhibits feature the works of local, national, and international artists). Scheduled for the Saturday closest to April Fool's Day, the center's annual Jell-O Show is a lighthearted and well-attended fundraiser with an open call for Jell-O creations and edible Jell-O contributions served at the tacky food buffet.

1910 E Fifteenth Ave.
541-345-1571
mkartcenter.org
artandthevineyard.org

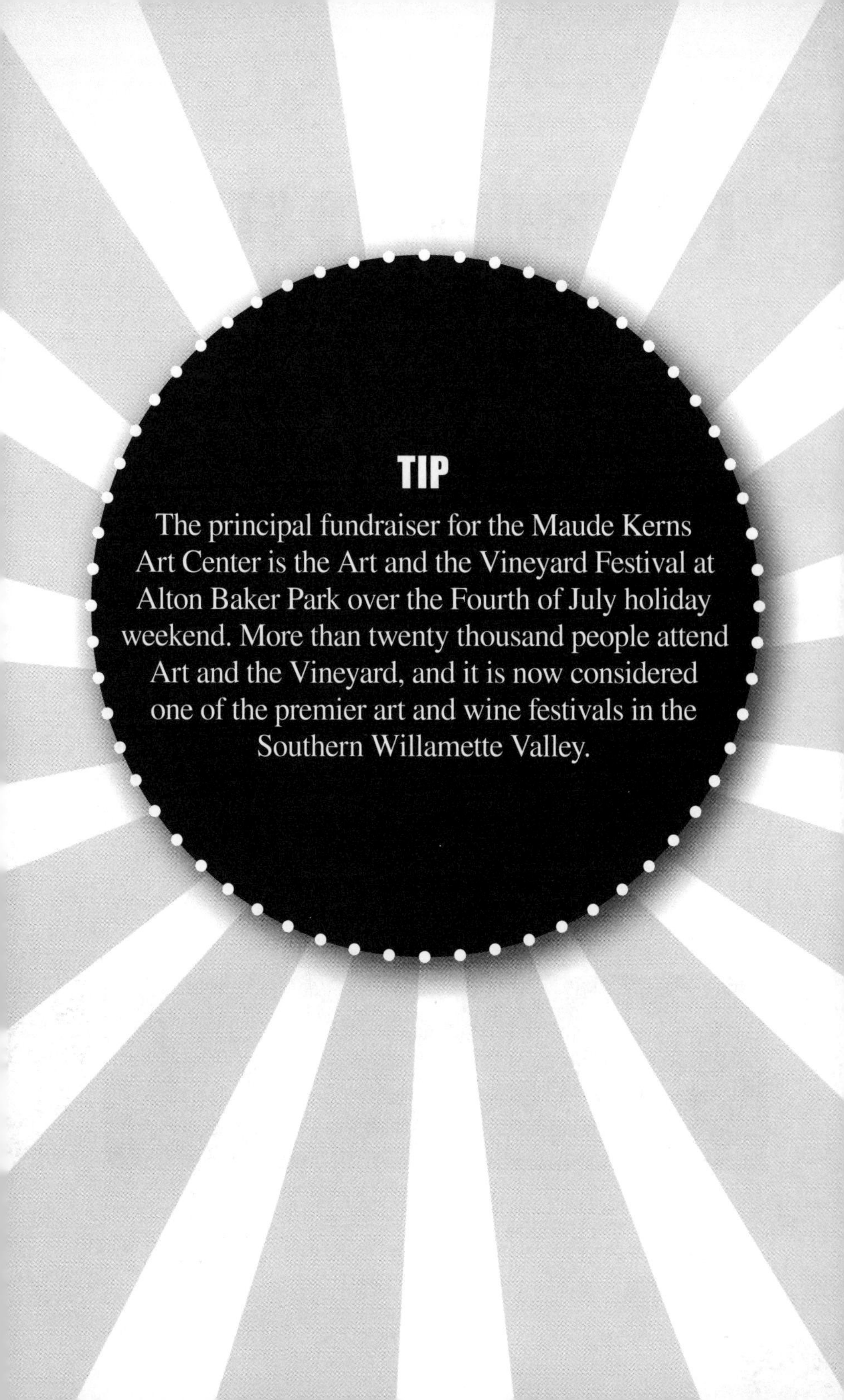

TIP

The principal fundraiser for the Maude Kerns Art Center is the Art and the Vineyard Festival at Alton Baker Park over the Fourth of July holiday weekend. More than twenty thousand people attend Art and the Vineyard, and it is now considered one of the premier art and wine festivals in the Southern Willamette Valley.

PAY TRIBUTE TO STEVE PREFONTAINE
AT PRE'S ROCK

Steve Roland "Pre" Prefontaine was an all-American middle- and long-distance runner born and raised in Coos Bay on the Oregon coast. A graduate of the University of Oregon, Pre remains a local legend in Eugene. Once the American record holder in seven different distance track events, from 2,000 meters to 10,000 meters, Pre competed in the 1972 Olympic Games in Munich, Germany, where he placed fourth in the 5,000-meter race. In training for the 1976 Montreal Olympics, Pre's life ended on May 30, 1975, in a fatal car crash on Skyline Boulevard just above the University District. Today, a memorial stone marks the site of the accident. Runners from near and far leave trinkets and items in Pre's memory, from running shoes to medals, race bibs, coins, and items of clothing.

Follow signs for Pre's Rock on Skyline Boulevard

TIP

If you seek out Pre's Rock, try the Hendricks Park route for a first-time visit. Park in the designated pullout a short distance from the memorial and watch for traffic in both directions.

FOR MORE WAYS TO PAY TRIBUTE TO STEVE PREFONTAINE IN EUGENE, VISIT THESE LOCAL SITES:

University of Oregon Hall of Champions and Hall of Fame: A collection of trophies and memorabilia from glorious moments in University of Oregon sports history.

The Old Pad (formerly the Paddock): A classic Eugene bar. Prefontaine worked here as a bartender in the early 1970s.

Prefontaine Classic: One of the premier track and field meets in the United States; held each year at Hayward Field at the University of Oregon.

Pre's Trail at Alton Baker Park: A four-mile long running and walking trail built in the fall of 1975 as a tribute to Prefontaine.

DUCKS

SHOPPING AND FASHION

DINE, SHOP, OR LEARN TO COOK

AT FIFTH STREET PUBLIC MARKET

Located at the corner of Fifth and High streets in downtown Eugene, Fifth Street Public Market occupies a full city block. Spanning three levels, the market's interior faces an open-air courtyard with a stately brick fountain as its focal point. Tenants range from cafés and restaurants to professional offices, fashion boutiques, jewelers, florists, home furnishings stores, and toy and gift stores. The cooking school within Provisions Market Hall on the main level is a popular gathering spot for local foodies. Running between 6 p.m. and 8 p.m. every Tuesday evening, mid-June through the end of September, the "Music at the Market" series features local musicians in the courtyard with extended dining hours at the international cafés. Out-of-towners have the option of booking a luxurious suite at the Inn at Fifth, a four-diamond boutique hotel and spa attached to the property.

296 E Fifth Ave., #300
541-484-0383
5stmarket.com

HUNT FOR DEALS WHILE DOING GOOD
AT S.A.R.A.'S TREASURES

One of the more unique business models in Eugene, S.A.R.A.'s Treasures is a combination thrift shop and animal shelter. Short for Shelter Animal Resource Alliance, since 2001 S.A.R.A.'s has saved nearly nine hundred cats that would otherwise have been euthanized at local shelters. It is a retail store located on River Road, and visitors shop for clothing, books, jewelry, and household items, as well as cat food and supplies. The real "treasure" of the shopping experience is interacting with the cats and kittens that live in oversized pens throughout the building—the pens are large enough for potential future pet owners to interact with the animals during their shopping experience. Proceeds from donated items benefit the animals; popular "parking lot sales" run between May and October and help keep the business and adoptions up and running.

871 River Rd.
541-607-8892
sarastreasures.org

IMPROVE THE PLANET
AT BRING RECYCLING CENTER

One of the greenest and most environmentally conscious cities in America, Eugene supports all the R's: Reducing, Reusing, Recycling, and Rethinking. Case in point: BRING Recycling Center on Franklin Boulevard—one of the nation's oldest non-profit recycling organizations—has been helping residents "live well without waste" since 1971. From salvage to surplus, BRING collects and resells building materials, appliances, garden tools, furniture, lumber, scrap metal, tile, tools, windows, and the list goes on and on. Customers pick through an expansive indoor, outdoor, and semi-enclosed retail space, unearthing treasures for their next home improvement, remodel, or creative art project. On the center's north side, edible and drought-resistant plants fill an 8,500-square-foot Garden of Earthly Delights (look for whimsical artwork created with porcelain toilet tank covers, rebar, and PVC piping), which serves as an outdoor workshop and community gathering space.

4446 Franklin Blvd.
541-746-3023
bringrecycling.org

DIG FOR TREASURES
AT PICC-A-DILLY FLEA MARKET

If one man's junk is another man's treasure, there's something for every man (and woman) at the Picc-A-Dilly Flea Market. Eugene's largest and longest-running flea market, Picc-A-Dilly has been drawing in the Eugene community since 1970. Housed inside the Lane County Fairgrounds livestock buildings, the flea market runs every other Sunday with the exception of July and August. Be prepared for crowds and crowded spaces, as the vendor tables span multiple aisles in three main rooms.

796 W Thirteenth Ave.
541-683-5589
piccadillyflea.com

TIP

If you're a hard-core picker, arrive by 8 a.m. for the best selection. Otherwise, note that the per-person admission price drops from $7.50 to $1.50 after 10 a.m.

STOCK UP ON GAG GIFTS
AT HIRONS DRUG

Hirons Drug is Eugene's most unique everything store and oldest locally owned pharmacy. Hirons has everything, from greeting cards to office supplies, wind chimes, inner tubes, feather boas, metal lunch boxes, and even inflatable unicorn horns for your cat. At least two aisles are dedicated to green and yellow paraphernalia in support of the Oregon Ducks. Hirons has two stores in Eugene, one on Eighteenth Avenue and one on Franklin Boulevard. Both locations house a legitimate pharmacy and official United States Post Office branch. While some people are drawn into the chaos of glitter and reflective tape, claustrophobic types may use words such as hives and panic to describe their Hirons shopping experience.

185 E Eighteenth Ave.
541-344-4832

1950 Franklin Blvd.
541-344-5260
hironsdrug.com

TIP
Subscribe to the Hirons email list for periodic coupons in your inbox.

EXPERIENCE THE HOLIDAY TREE LIGHTING
AT OAKWAY CENTER

Branded as a "lifestyle center and premier shopping experience," Oakway Center is one of three area shopping malls. Primarily spanning a triangle of land between Coburg Road, Oakway Road, and Oakmont Way, the fifty-five-year-old shopping district houses a blend of restaurants, cafés, retail stores, businesses, and personal care services. At the center of Oakway Center is Heritage Courtyard, an outdoor courtyard where visitors are encouraged to congregate in the mix of green space, oak trees, an Italian-style fountain, and a paved entertainment area. A holiday tradition for the past thirty years, the annual Oakway Center Tree Lighting Celebration occurs in late November. Families in particular look forward to hot chocolate, live music, real reindeer, and celebrity guests like Winter Willy the Snowman.

2350 Oakmont Way, #204
541-485-4711
oakwaycenter.com

95

EXPLORE
UP AND DOWN WILLAMETTE STREET

Running six and a half miles between the Amtrak station in downtown Eugene and Fox Hollow Road past the Spencer Butte trailhead, Willamette Street is the physical north-south dividing line between addresses in East and West Eugene. It is lined on both sides by many stores, restaurants, residences, businesses, and places of industry and worship. Noteworthy points of interest along Willamette Street include gilt+gossamer, Shoe-A-Holic, Dot Dotson's Photo Finishing, Tsunami Books, Metropol Bakery, Off the Waffle, and Capella Market. It is best explored on foot or with two wheels; be prepared to make more stops than you anticipate.

CHANNEL BOB MARLEY
AT LAZAR'S BAZAR

One of the most colorful novelty shops in Eugene, Lazar's Bazar sells everything you need to assimilate into the city's hippie culture: hand-blown glass, incense, oils, henna, band posters, beads and jewelry, lava lamps, flags, and t-shirts ranging from tie dye to political statements. It has been in business for over forty years. Owner Lazar Makyadath made headlines when he ran for Eugene mayor in 2000. "Lazar for Mayor" bumper stickers are periodically spotted around town. It embraces the advertising slogan "the store your mother warned you about," but many of the items sold at Lazar's Bazar became less taboo after Oregon voters passed a measure to legalize the sale and consumption of recreational marijuana in 2014. While Lazar's does not sell cannabis, it specializes in kratom, an herb in the coffee family used to combat pain, depression, and anxiety.

57 W Broadway
541-687-0139
lazarseugene.com

97

DRESS TO IMPRESS
AT TRILLIUM AND OF THE EARTH

When it comes to dressing to impress, one way to break the mold is to consciously select sustainability and quality over mass production and bargain pricing. Sourcing high-quality, natural fabrics ranging from hemp to organic cotton, bamboo, tencel, and even recycled water bottles, both Trillium and Of the Earth tap into a network of makers and artists to create the many clothing items, pieces of jewelry, and accessories on the shelves in their stores. Trillium, located in South Eugene, offers a range of clothing options for men, women, and children. Of the Earth offers similar choices, with an emphasis on earth-inspired colors in both its online store and retail storefront on Blair Boulevard in the Whiteaker neighborhood.

Trillium Clothing Store
3235 Donald St.
541-485-8117
trilliumclothingstore.com

Of the Earth
782 Blair Blvd.
541-543-7195
oftheearth.com

LOAD UP ON DUCKS GEAR
IN THE UNIVERSITY DISTRICT

Aptly known as the University Shopping District, the stores framing both sides of East Thirteenth Avenue leading into the University of Oregon cater to the college crowd. From cookie dough to pizza, frozen yogurt, fast food, beer, and coffee, this close-to-campus hub of commerce is teeming with pedestrians all year round. Not surprisingly, a behemoth campus bookstore, the Duck Store, occupies the corner of East Thirteenth Avenue and Kincaid Street. Teeming with athletic gear, office supplies, textbooks, and electronic gadgets, the upper-level bookstore features a corner designed with kids in mind.

RELIVE YOUR CHILDHOOD
AT REPLAY TOYS

An independently owned local toy store, Replay Toys has a unique business model—most everything is used, vintage, or a combination of the two. It seeks to provide a place where kids, parents, and collectors can recycle or reuse toys at fair prices, and Transformers, Star Wars, Power Rangers, My Little Pony, and Teenage Mutant Ninja Turtles are common inventory lining the shelves in the small retail space in South Eugene. Replay is also Eugene's premier location for Legos and Lego minifigures, with collectible characters or the option to build your own (look for the Lego table with the option to pay for individual pieces a la carte or by the pound).

255 E Eighteenth Ave.
541-782-8711

TIP

When selling items to Replay, customers have the option to cash out or earn store credit, with store credit typically yielding a higher dollar amount.

CREATE AN UPCYCLED ART PROJECT
AT MECCA

Valuing Earth, creativity, and community, MECCA (Materials Exchange Center for Community Arts) helps to divert scrap material out of the waste stream and into creative endeavors across Eugene. Located near the Amtrak train station in downtown Eugene, MECCA accepts donations of nearly any and all art supplies (think ribbon, glitter, paint, clay, corks, shells, stickers, yarn, and picture frames) and sells them back to the community at a reasonable price. Sometimes prices are "make an offer," with free supplies for educators and non-profits in the Teacher Resource Center. Beyond the eclectic and whimsical variety of supplies for purchase, MECCA's studio space is available to anyone without the space at home to create and complete art projects (the space is open to the general public on a pay-what-you-can basis; groups and crafting parties are welcome).

449 Willamette St.
541-302-1810
materials-exchange.org

SUGGESTED ITINERARIES

SPORTS LOVER

WITH THE FAMILY

NATURE IS CALLING

ESSENTIAL EUGENE

DATE NIGHT

SAVE THE PLANET

EDUCATIONAL ADVENTURE

ACTIVITIES
BY SEASON

SPRING

SUMMER

FALL

WINTER

INDEX